步步为营

跨文化商务沟通实战

（学生用书）

朱春飞 主编

DOING BUSINESS ACROSS CULTURES

Effective Communication

浙江工商大學出版社
ZHEJIANG GONGSHANG UNIVERSITY PRESS
·杭州·

图书在版编目(CIP)数据

步步为营：跨文化商务沟通实战 / 朱春飞主编.
— 杭州：浙江工商大学出版社，2020.6
ISBN 978-7-5178-3900-2

Ⅰ.①步… Ⅱ.①朱… Ⅲ.①商业管理—公共关系学
—高等职业教育—教材 Ⅳ.①F715

中国版本图书馆CIP数据核字(2020)第097804号

Doing Business across Cultures: Effective Communication
步步为营：跨文化商务沟通实战
BUBU WEI YING: KUA WENHUA SHANGWU GOUTONG SHIZHAN
朱春飞 主编

责任编辑 王黎明
责任校对 张春琴
封面设计 林朦朦
责任印制 包建辉
出版发行 浙江工商大学出版社
(杭州市教工路198号 邮政编码310012)
(E-mail：zjgsupress@163.com)
(网址：http://www.zjgsupress.com)
电话：0571-88904980，88831806（传真）
排　　版 杭州红羽文化创意有限公司
印　　刷 浙江全能工艺美术印刷有限公司
开　　本 787 mm×1092 mm 1/16
印　　张 14
字　　数 247千
版 印 次 2020年6月第1版 2020年6月第1次印刷
书　　号 ISBN 978-7-5178-3900-2
定　　价 58.00元

浙江工商大学出版社营销部邮购电话 0571—88904970

内容提要

NEIRONG TIYAO

本数字化教材在广泛采集外贸企业案例的基础上开发相关的工作任务，并把外贸业务沟通流程和出口产品知识相整合，具有“实用性、拓展性、话题式、职场化、任务化”的特点。本数字化教材内容主要包括：参加国际展会、接待客户企业拜访、沟通价格、商务用餐、沟通品质、沟通包装、沟通装运、沟通保险、沟通支付、沟通合同签约、沟通海外代理、沟通投诉等12个工作情境。

本书可以作为高等院校、职业院校国际经济与贸易、国际贸易实务、商务英语等专业的教材，也可以作为外贸从业人员的业务参考用书及培训用书。

前言

QIANYAN

当下，作为世界工厂的中国制造面临着转型升级、国际市场风云变化的挑战，外贸行业对业务员职业能力提出了更高的要求，我们制造企业尤其是中小企业，特别需要诚信、勤奋、专业、创新、敬业、好学尤其是善于沟通的外贸人才，助力中国制造继续进军国际市场。

本数字化教材依托于一线采集的外贸企业案例开发相关的工作任务，并把外贸业务沟通流程和出口产品知识进行整合，内容涵盖参加国际展会、接待客户拜访企业、沟通价格、商务用餐、沟通品质、沟通包装、沟通装运、沟通保险、沟通支付、沟通合同签约、沟通海外代理、沟通投诉等12个工作情境。在这12工作情景下本书开发了相关的学习任务，主要包括：①认识工作情境；②介绍出口案例产品；③体验商务沟通案例；④理解沟通案例；⑤分析出口国市场及客户；⑥分析拓展案例；⑦模拟相关沟通任务。本书以跨文化的视角分析国际商务沟通活动，有助于学生更好地了解出口产品、了解目标市场、了解中小外贸企业的工作任务，培养“客户至上”的服务精神、助力中国制造“走出去”。

本教材通过数字化手段把外贸企业典型案例充分地呈现、分析，从而实现了引入企业专家及企业资源，拓展了学生的学习空间、深化了学生的职场“体验”。同时，在数字化资源的支持下课堂翻转为以“学生为学习主体”的体验式学习：学生主持和进行口头汇报，学生拍摄小组情景表演，学习小组以既定的任务清单模拟商务沟通任务。此外，我们的数字化教材还支持在学堂在线、浙江省高等学校在线开放课程共享平台、超星学银平台的慕课学习，而且学生可以自由选择合适的平台并通过在线平台的测验、上传分享、发帖、讨论等功能，促进同班、跨班、跨年级的同伴以及慕课平台同伴学习成果的展示、比较和交流，从而建构线上的“学习共同体”，让学生在比较、关注、参与、竞争、体验、互助中不断提升学习的积极性和主动性。

本数字化教材充分发挥了企业教师在课程建设中的主体作用，前后有近30位资深的外贸从业人员参与了课程前期的开发、设计，在转化为数字化资源的过程中有14位外贸从业人员参与了撰稿、讲授、拍摄及制作。在此特别感谢参与了本数字化教材撰稿、讲授、拍摄及制作的企业嘉宾：海宁先科新材料科技有限公司外贸经理张逸佳、杭州江南服饰有限公司业务经理杜艳、杭州兴禾进出口有限公司销售经理章晓霞、杭州富阳鸿美玩具有限公司业务部经理万美君、长兴经纬竹制品有限公司外贸业务员沈玉琪、浙江金纺贸易有限公司副总经理宋泉锋、金石集团业务经理曹莉娜和吴晓庆、嘉兴德永纺织品有限公司营业部部长王玉叶和业务员罗丹琴、杭州赛丽进出口有限公司业务组长熊迎迎、杭州冠隆服饰有限公司外贸业务员王玲。此外，特别感谢如下企业人士为数字化教材提供的案例、建议、相关出口产品等：桐庐龙龙进出口有限公司李婷、浙江金中机电科技有限公司外贸部主管沈建红、义乌紫尚进出口公司经理胡燕紫、浙江东晓文具有限公司外销经理陈熙、永康多嘉盛有限公司业务员马文思、杭州赛顺机电设备有限公司业务经理许周洁、义乌九州长和国际贸易有限公司总经理卢胜德、浙江永康王琪涵先生等。此外，特别感谢杭州言坤科技有限公司吴淑丽等后期的精心制作、浙江工商大学出版社王黎明编辑给予的无私帮助和大力支持。

本数字化教材在编写过程中得到了浙江机电职业技术学院教务处、数字贸易学院给予的指导、支持和经费资助，创意设计学院给予拍摄场地的支持，在此表达最诚挚的谢意。同时，本书在编写过程中参考和借鉴了同行的成果，在此表达由衷的感谢。

由于时间、水平有限，本书难免有不足之处，还希望广大专家、同学能够对本书的不当之处给以批评和指正。

朱春飞

2020年6月于杭州

目录

项目1 参加国际展会

学习目标

知识目标

1. 了解国际展会的概况、作用；
2. 理解国际展会沟通的要点和难点；
3. 掌握参加国际展会的英语表述和沟通策略。

能力目标

1. 能够搜集国际展会相关的资料；
2. 掌握如何同参展的目标国客户进行有效沟通；
3. 明确参展任务的要点并完成情景模拟任务。

任务1.1 认识国际展会

展会从字面上理解是供陈列、观看的聚会，也是在集市、庙会形式上发展起来的高层次的展览形式。展会在英语里有fair、exhibition、exposition、show等表述方式。一般而言，专业的展会在固定或一系列的地点、特定的日期和期限里举行，通过展示达到产品、服务以及信息的交流。在近现代，国际性的展会对于出口型的企业而言作用和价值不容小觑。

> 根据上述的介绍，请你完成如下的学习任务：

❶ 列举展会的作用：

❷ 归纳展会对参展者的能力要求：

❸ 列举5个国际展会（中英文对照、备注举办地）：

1.	
2.	
3.	
4.	
5.	

任务1.2 分析展会沟通案例

1.2.1 介绍案例产品：儿童滑板车

儿童滑板车（kids scooter）作为一款儿童玩具，不仅能锻炼儿童身体的灵活性，而且还可以增强他们的体质，深受国内外小朋友的喜爱。虽然儿童滑板车整体构造简单，但是出口企业要根据目标客户及市场的需求不断改进设计、采用不同的材质、申请相关的认证。目前，国内儿童滑板车比较知名的生产厂家主要集中在浙江永康一带。

> 根据上述的介绍，请你完成如下的学习任务：

❶ 概括儿童滑板车的构造：

❷ 搜集滑板车的材质信息：

1. T把	
2. 踏板	
3. 轮子	

❸ 罗列出口市场特点：

1.

2.

3.

❹ 归纳产品主要的出口认证：

❺ 补充案例产品信息：

扫一扫

1.2.2 展会的沟通案例

【案例背景介绍】

浙江永康的一家专业生产儿童滑板车的企业派业务员Jessica和Emma参加广交会。Jessica是公司资深的业务员，有丰富的从业经验；而Emma是从学校毕业不久的新人，出发前公司对她做了必要的培训，并希望通过这次展会培养和历练她。下面我们一起来分享她们在展会上如何接待来自德国的客商Daniel。

Jessica: Good afternoon. Welcome to our booth. I'm Jessica and this is my colleague, Emma.

Daniel: Hello, thanks. I'm Daniel. Nice to meet you.

Emma: Nice to meet you too. Daniel, please take a look at our samples.

Daniel: Are you a trader or a manufacturer?

Jessica: A manufacturer. And what products are you looking for?

Daniel: For kids scooters.

Jessica: As for kids scooters, we have many patterns. Would you like to know more? Take a seat if you like.

Daniel: Thanks! Have you ever exported them to Germany?

Jessica: Yes, of course.

Daniel: Who are your clients in Germany?

Jessica: Norma.

Daniel: Ok, I see.

Emma: Would you like coffee or tea, Daniel?

Daniel: Er, coffee for me, please.

Jessica: Daniel, there are classical patterns and new patterns for kids scooters from page 4 to 28 of the catalogue. If you want to know more about the products you are interested in, please let me know.

Emma: This is coffee and water for you, Daniel.

Daniel: Great! Thanks, Emma.

Emma: You are welcome.

Daniel: Do you have the certificate of GS?

Emma: Now our company has passed ISO9001, CE, RoHS, and BSCI. If you ask for GS, we can apply for it.

Daniel: Oh, good. And I like this pattern.

Jessica: This pattern is selling quite well. Besides, the wheels of KM-9513 are with music, and the ones of KM-9514 will flash.

Daniel: And here is a safety question. I want to know the distance between the wheels and the T-bar.

Jessica: Don't worry. Children's fingers will not be allowed to put into this gap.

Daniel: Ok, good. What's the price?

Jessica: Do you want aluminum or steel?

Daniel: 100% aluminum，please.

Emma: You'd better tell us your quantity too.

Daniel: I would like to start with 8, 000 PCS.

Jessica: We will contact with our boss. As you know the prices of materials are changing. Please wait a moment.

Jessica: Is there any more information you want to know?

Daniel: How soon could you deliver the goods?

Jessica: Well，we can deliver you the products within 1 month after you pay the 30% deposit.

Jessica: We have checked with our boss. Our quotation is 8 dollars per unit FOB Shanghai according to your quantity.

Daniel: By the way，could you give me a discount if I place the order at this trade fair?

Jessica: Well，according to our usual practice，we can give you 5% off.

Daniel: Thank you. I will contact with you afterwards.

Jessica: This is our business card and catalogue. We will be here for 5 days. So if you have time，please come and visit us. May I have your business card?

Daniel: Yes，of course. Here you are. See you.

Emma & Jessica: Thank you. See you.

> 根据上述的案例，请你完成如下的学习任务：

❶ 请把加框的单词填入表格并注上中文，并把画线的句子翻译在原文处。

1.	2.	3.	4.
5.	6.	7.	8.
9.	10.	11.	12.

❷ 重点跟读加框的单词、画线的句子并能准确、流利地读出来、说出来。

1.2.3 理解展会沟通案例

亲爱的同学们，很多出口企业仍然选择通过各类展会拓展国际市场。展会为国际买家、制造商以及中间商提供了面对面沟通和交流的平台，在对外贸易中依然发挥着重要的作用。我们有很多同学可能在工作不久后就会被公司派去参加各类展会。不少同学都特别担心，“我的英语可以吗”“我要讲什么啊”。请大家跟随我们的课程一起来学习，看看是否真的有这么难。

> 根据上述的介绍，请你完成如下的学习任务：

❶ 归纳同国外客人熟识的步骤：

❷ 分析采集和识别客人信息的方法：

❸ 总结客户 Daniel 需求：

❹ 归纳展会的推销技巧：

❺ 分析参展跟进客户的方法：

扫一扫

1.2.4 分析德国市场及客户

德国地处欧洲大陆的十字路口，也是欧洲邻国最多、欧盟人口最多的国家。优越的地缘政治决定了德国的市场地位，也为德国开拓贸易关系提供良好的先天基础。我们一提到德国人，就会联想到理性、严谨、认真、守时、讲信誉、守纪律等等。历史上，德国的诗人、学者层出不穷，被誉为“诗人与思想家的国家”，比如歌德、海涅、康德、黑格尔。德国虽历经两次世界大战的惨败，但又凤凰涅槃、再次迅速崛起，一跃成为世界经济大国。

> 根据上述的介绍，请你完成如下的学习任务：

❶ 罗列德国概况：

❷ 分析德国消费者需求特点：

❸ 分析德国客户特点：

❹ 谈谈本视频给予你的启发：

❺ 补充德国市场及客户分析：

任务1.3 分析拓展案例：展会是否还要参加？

随着电子商务的普及、全球电商市场的发展，很多人开始质疑：我们是否还要去参加展会？德国某个运动展的数据显示：三年间共有7863家企业参展，其中4730家企业三年间只参加了一次，其余的企业则是多次参展。换言之，不少企业选择了连续参加展会。那么，关于参展话题让我们一起来听听外贸人的观点吧。

> 根据上述的介绍，请你完成如下的学习任务：

❶ 分析外贸人的观点：

1. Cathy	
2. Lucy	
3. Sally	

❷ 概括参展企业的做法：

❸ 分析参展的作用：

❹ 谈谈拓展案例给予你的启发：

❺ 简述你对展会的看法：

任务1.4 模拟展会沟通任务

1.4.1 模拟展会产品介绍任务

大家今后在工作中主要从事商品出口贸易，因此了解、熟悉产品并能用英语专业、到位地表述出来非常重要。那么如何对一款出口产品做简要的介绍呢？

暑期在外贸企业实习的同学可以结合相关企业的产品，其他同学则可以结合自己的兴趣、你们当地特色/优势出口产品等完成本学习任务。

选定产品后，就要多方面采集有关这个产品的相关信息。这些信息主要包括正确的英语产品名称、消费群体、主要材质及功能、操作方法等。在信息搜索过程中，我们建议，先搜索中文的信息，对上述几个方面有了比较全面、深入的了解后，再根据产品正确的英文名称搜集产品的英文信息。

【参考例文】

My Product Presented at the Trade Fair

Good morning， ladies and gentleman. I'm Susan from DD Electronic Scale Factory. I will introduce you our new product—talking kitchen scale.

It is offered for the blind and those with low vision. And it is mainly made of steel and plastics. First，this product is convenient for operation. It speaks prompts and results in a clear female voice in your choice of English or Spanish. Look，with the flip of a switch on the back of the scale，you can turn off the talking function. Weights are also displayed on the clear LCD readout. Choose pounds，kilograms，grams，or ounces as you need. Besides，tare function assures accurate measurements，and it lets you weigh the food only.

Second，it is easy for maintenance. You just use one 9-Volt Battery (included) and it can shut off by itself so it conserves battery. When you want to clean it，you just wash the bowl in the dishwasher, and the rest can be cleaned with a damp cloth.

Finally, I want to add that our factory have Certificates of CE, RoHS, BSCI and ISO9001. Thanks for your attention. Any questions?

> 根据上述的介绍，请你完成如下的学习任务：

记录同学有关展会产品介绍的汇报要点：

Reporter:	Name of product:
Detailed information	1. 2. 3.
I suggest	
I ask	
I learn	

备注：欢迎大家登录课程的在线平台，点击观看往届学生的任务展示及教师点评。

扫一扫

1.4.2 模拟展会上同国外客户沟通的任务

学习小组将根据课程的学习，模拟参展商和外国客户在广交会的情景下交流和沟通。要求具体如下：①参展商和客户要了解对方的背景信息；同时，就产品的材质、功能、认证证书、价格、货期等展开交流和沟通。

②准备相关的样品、目录册、报价单等资料等及茶水，有些材料也可以通过手提电脑来展示。

③佩戴参展商及采购商的代表证，正装出镜。

④在任务中脱稿表演。

⑤选取或布置有展会背景的场地进行本情景表演拍摄。

> 根据上述的介绍，请你完成如下的学习任务：

记录有关小组参展沟通任务的要点：

The team:	Name of product:
Detailed information	1. 2. 3.
I suggest	
I ask	
I learn	

备注：欢迎大家登录课程的在线平台，点击观看往届学生的任务展示及教师点评。

扫一扫

1.4.3 模拟参展的即兴任务

这个任务中模拟广交会的客户开发的工作任务。由教师扮演的参展客户来到你们的摊位，他/她会关注产品的功能、操作、材料（function、operation、material）等。重点请关注客户想要了解的订单的基本信息（例如：price、minimum order quantity、certificates 等），以及留下同客人联络的方式。在本即兴表演中，教师会配合你们团队完成客户信息采集。希望团队成员在现场同潜在客户沟通中能让客人留下良好而深刻的印象。

> 根据上述的介绍，请你完成如下的学习任务：

❶ 团队根据分配到的任务编号学习相关的产品信息单。

❷ 团队分配任务，搜集该产品相关的文字和图片资料，并准备可能的展会资料及用品。

❸ 团队在即兴任务的完成过程中，及时采集客户的信息并完成如下信息表。

The Mini-file about This Buyer		
Photo	The product	
	Price quoted	
	Delivery	
	Quantity	
	Address	
Name:	Email	
Nationality:	Organization	
Notes:		

❹ 在即兴任务进行时，请在同伴小组的任务单下记录相关的信息并做必要的评价。

> 即兴任务附件

No.1

Battery Bottle Opener

Insert a long needle through the cork(软木塞) and into the bottle, then press a button.
Your bottle is opened. It's a simple and fast way to open a bottle!
One cartridge(钻头) can open 60–80 bottles.
Price: USD14 per piece FOB Shanghai
MOQ: 1, 000 PCS
Certificates: CE, GS

No.2

Fruit Metal Peeler

It can peel the fruit quickly and smoothly.
Thickened blade(刀片) and nonskid(防滑) hand shank make it superior!!!
Power supply: manual peeler
Blade material: stainless steel
Weight: 4 g
Length: 19 cm
Price: USD1.5 per piece FOB Ningbo
MOQ: 2, 000 PCS
Certificates: ISO9001, ISO14000, BSCI

No.3

Kid Scooter

It can make the kids move fast and safely.

Strong wheels make it safe and the body with Aluminum + Iron goes fast and lightly!!!

Recommended age: Above 3 years

Product size: 60 cm*9.4 cm*(52–76) cm

Net Weight: 3 kgs

Wheels: 125 mm PU wheel

Price: USD11 per piece FOB Zhanjiang Port

MOQ: 2, 000 PCS

Certificates: CE, RoHS, ISO9001

No.4

Automatic Straight Umbrella

It can offer full coverage and is large enough to protect you and your lover.

The button is on the handle, and it makes easier for you to open the umbrella!!!

Type: Rain-shade, not anti UV

Product size: 23”*8K

Material: 100% polyester.

Price: 5 USD per piece FOB Shanghai Port

MOQ: 500 PCS

Certificates: ISO9001, BSCI, Sedex

No.5

USB Flash Drive

It can support different types of OS(操作系统).

Durable data storage and fast speed in write/read transfer!!!

Material: metal

Capacity: 32 MB to 256 GB

Lifetime :over 1 million times

Weight: 30 grams

Price: USD0.5–25 per piece FOB Zhanjiang Port

MOQ: 1, 000 PCS

Certificates: ISO9001, ISO14001, BSCI

No.6

Foldable LED Desk Lamp

It will save over 80% on electricity bill of lighting.

Good for your eyes!!!

Switch function: Low/Middle/High/Off

Material: aluminum(铝)

Including a USB line

Recommended age: Above 5 years

Price: USD6 per piece FOB Putian Port

MOQ: 800 PCS

Certificates: ISO9001, ISO14001, CE, UL

项目2 接待客户企业拜访

学习目标

知识目标

1. 了解客户企业拜访的作用、价值；
2. 理解客户企业拜访的要点和难点；
3. 掌握接待客户企业拜访的英语表述和沟通策略。

能力目标

1. 能够搜集客户公司拜访相关的资料；
2. 掌握如何同目标国客户就公司拜访进行有效的商务沟通；
3. 明确接待客户公司拜访的要点并完成模拟任务。

扫一扫

任务 2.1 认识客户企业拜访

国外新客户确定来企业拜访说明了对方想更进一步地了解企业、产品，这也是为双方下单、或者说下大订单做准备。对于初次来访的国外客户，我们一方面要尽可能搜集客户信息及其企业参观、拜访的具体要求，另一方面也要有针对性地进行准备从而更好地开启今后的合作。对于老客户的来访，我们既要根据客户以往的拜访要求，又要结合其新需求进行准备，在维护双方已有的合作关系、信任关系的基础上进一步拓展业务。

> 根据上述的介绍，请你完成如下的学习任务：

❶ 分析客户拜访的要求：

新客户	老客户

❷ 概括客户参观工厂的注意点：

❸ 分析亲赴机场接客户的原因：

任务2.2 分析客户企业拜访沟通案例

扫一扫

2.2.1 介绍案例产品：出口笔

在中国，制笔业形成了门类完善、品种多样的生产体系，制笔企业达到了3000余家，从业人员近20万。当下，中国的制笔行业在国内外消费需求的共同推动下呈现出新的生机与活力，成为世界最大的笔类生产与出口大国。中国的制笔企业在激烈的国内外市场竞争中不断成长，积极提升自身的出口竞争实力。目前，仅在宁波、杭州桐庐、丽水庆元等地就形成了规模大、专业性强的出口基地。

> 根据上述的介绍，请你完成如下的学习任务：

❶ 罗列笔的基本构造：

❷ 分析产品种类及其材质：

1.	
2.	
3.	

❸ 总结出口市场的特点：

1.

2.

3.

……

❹ 评价产品介绍的方法：

2.2.2 客户企业拜访的沟通案例

扫一扫

【案例背景介绍】

浙江桐庐的一家专业生产圆珠笔的企业接待了来自土耳其的新客户。Wendy是公司资深的业务员，公司安排让她负责客户Halwest全程的拜访活动。在本案例中，Wendy在约定地点接到了客户并亲自陪伴客户参观了工厂。下面我们一起来分享她如何接待客户拜访。

Wendy: Hello, Halwest?

Halwest: Yes.

Wendy: I'm Wendy from Feida Pen Manufactory Company. Welcome to Tonglu, and this way please. Our car is just over there. Can I help you with your luggage?

Halwest: Thank you, Wendy.

Wendy: How about your flight, Halwest?

Halwest: It was good.

Wendy: Be careful.

Wendy: Is your order for promotion or stationery?

Halwest: Well, just for stationery. And what are your main products?

Wendy: We manufacture a vast range of pens, mainly including office pens, business gifts and promotional pens. At present, our factory has a product range of 150 models in 20 lines. And what products are you most interested in?

Halwest: Business gifts.

Wendy: Oh, I see.

Wendy: Here we are, and this is our factory. First, let's have a look around?

Halwest: Oh, that's great.

Wendy: This way please.

Halwest: How many workers do you have?

Wendy: About four hundred full-time. We take on casual staff if necessary.

Halwest: Which country do you export to?

Wendy: We export our products to America, Russia, Turkey and Asian countries.

Halwest: Great! Do you know New Life in Turkey? Do they have orders with you?

Wendy: Yeah, we have cooperated with them several times.

Halwest: How about their orders? Can you show me their samples?

Wendy: Er, if you want to know, we can check and show you later on. Those are our workshops.

Halwest: This is really what I want to see. Thank you very much.

Wendy: Now we will visit Group 1 to watch the process of assembling metal pens.

Wendy: Look, our assembling starts here. And then the parts are fixed one by one.

Halwest: Thank you very much for your introduction. What is your best selling product this year?

Wendy: It's my pleasure. Next I will show it to you in our sample room and shall we go there for a further talk?

Halwest: Yes, of course. Let's go.

> 根据上述的案例，请你完成如下的学习任务：

❶ 请把加框的单词填入表格并注上中文，并把画线的句子翻译在原文处。

1.	2.	3.	4.
5.	6.	7.	8.

❷ 重点跟读加框的单词、画线的句子并能准确、流利地读出来、说出来。

扫一扫

2.2.3 理解客户企业拜访沟通案例

客人通过展会、网站认识和了解了我们的企业后，不少客人会选择通过小额的订单来试探企业的实际生产能力和服务水平，这个我们称为试单。如果试单进展顺利，说明已经初步赢得了客人的信任。那么，接下来有的客人就有可能选择实地参观工厂。如何顺利地完成新客人的工厂参观的接待任务呢？请大家跟随我们的课程一起进入今天的学习内容。

> 根据上述的介绍，请你完成如下的学习任务：

❶ 介绍在机场、车站接客人的准备：

❷ 评价 Wendy 应对客人打听竞争者信息的策略：

❸ 概括客人参观工厂时的关注点：

扫扫

2.2.4 分析土耳其市场及客户

土耳其横跨欧亚大陆，享有6500年的悠久历史、13个不同文明的历史遗产，被誉为“文明的摇篮”。20世纪80年代，土耳其实行对外开放政策，经济实现了跨越式发展，从经济基础较为落后的传统农业国向现代工业国迅速转变。我们一提到土耳其，就会联想到伊斯兰教、突厥后人、美食、浓郁的异域风情等等。今天，土耳其在多种文化，新与旧、东方与西方、现代与传统的融合中不断繁荣和发展。

› 根据上述的介绍，请你完成如下的学习任务：

❶ 列举土耳其的概况：

❷ 分析土耳其消费者需求特点：

❸ 分析土耳其客户特点：

❹ 谈谈本视频给予你的启发：

❺ 补充土耳其市场及客户分析：

任务 2.3 分析客户企业拜访拓展案例

扫一扫

在国外客户的开发中，客人提出到公司拜访往往表明客人有比较强的合作意向和诚意。Helen 在毕业实习的时候找了一家杭州的外贸服装企业，她凭借自己的用心和勤奋一手开发日本客人，而客人提出在 5 月份来公司拜访。下面，我们和大家分享这位外贸新人接待客人拜访的案例，希望这则小案例能带给大家一些启发和思考。

> 根据上述的介绍，请你完成如下的学习任务：

❶ 简述日本客人拜访时对 Helen 所在公司的要求：

❷ 总结客人拜访时的注意点：

1.

2.

3.

❸ 分析四家公司客户公司拜访的细节：

公司 1	
公司 2	
公司 3	
公司 4	

❹ 谈谈拓展案例给予你的启发：

任务 2.4 模拟接待客户拜访沟通任务

2.4.1 模拟介绍出口企业的任务

同学们，如果大家今后就职于外贸公司或外贸工厂，在日常工作中会碰到向国外客户介绍就职的企业。那么，有关外贸公司或外贸工厂的介绍应包括哪些方面？如何用英语专业、到位地进行介绍呢？

首先，暑期在外贸公司/工厂工作的同学可以介绍实习的企业，其他同学则可以结合自己的兴趣、地方出口企业进行介绍。但是，这里我们要提醒大家，我们要求大家介绍的是出口型的中小企业，请不要选择例如KFC、IBM、华为，虽然这些企业的确很大、英语资料很多，但不是我们的目标企业。企业锁定后，就要多方面采集有关这个企业的相关信息。路径很多，比如，进入企业官网查中英文介绍；或者进入面向出口的专业网站（http：//www.made-in-china.com/；https：//www.amazon.com/；https：//www.alibaba.com），了解更多的企业资讯。

其次，有关一家外贸企业的介绍往往会包括如下这些方面：

①公司的名称（e.g., Ningbo Newstar Garment Co., Ltd.）

成立及出口时间（e.g., Our factory was founded in 1998 and we started exporting in 2005.）

地理位置（e.g., Our factory is located in Fuzhou, China.）

邻近的港口及机场（e.g., It is closely next to Shanghai Port and Ningbo Port.）

②主要出口产品（e.g., Our main products include bike, bicycle, fix gear bike, electric bike, e-bike, and mountain bike.）

主要出口市场（e.g., Most of our products are exported to USA, Australia, Europe, and Asia.）

③生产能力（e.g., Our Annual production capacity is 250, 000 sets.）

研发生产能力（e.g., We are capable of OEM&ODM.）

员工组成（e.g., We have 300 full-time workers and 28 technicians.）

④主要出口的资质（e.g., We have the certificates of ISO9001, SA8000, GS, and BSCI.）

【参考例文】

A Brief Introduction to Our Company

Good morning, ladies and gentlemen. I'm XXX. I will introduce XXX company.

Our company is an international trade limited company established in 1990. It is located in Hefei, Anhui Province. There are 150 full-time employees in our company, of whom over 20 are high-ranking management personnel and over 30 are all talents with high technical titles.

We simply handle import and export trade on glass bottle, glass jar, glass bottle with stainless steel dispenser, plastic cap, and metal cap. Our main markets include

United States, Japan, the Middle East, Korea, and Southeast Asia. Our total annual sales volume is $16 million–$17 million.

We have our own stable base for raw materials and products. We also have several high level specialists and professors to guarantee the stability for our products. Besides, our have the certificates of FDA issued by SGS and Intertek. We can accept small orders; meanwhile, we provide customization work. We are willing to make friends domestically and overseas, and offer qualified products and services to all of our clients.

Thanks for your attention. Any questions?

> 根据上述的介绍，请你完成如下的学习任务：

记录同学企业介绍的汇报要点：

Reporter:	Name of company:
Detailed information	1. 2. 3.
I suggest	
I ask	
I learn	

备注：欢迎大家登录课程的在线平台，点击观看往届学生的任务展示及教师点评。

2.4.2　模拟接待客户初次拜访的任务

在本学习任务中，每个分配到任务的学习小组将根据课程的学习，模拟和前来拜访的外国客户在公司/工厂情景下交流和沟通。要求具体如下：

①双方如果是在外贸公司沟通，交流的信息侧重在产品范围、公司的出口资质、专业服务、出口市场、发货期等方面；双方如果是在外贸工厂沟通，交流的信息侧重在企业的生产能力、技术能力、员工情况、生产管理、出口资质、产品种类、出口市场等方面；

②准备相关的资料，有些材料也可以通过手提电脑等来展示；

③出口商佩戴工作证，双方请穿着正装出镜；

④请在任务中脱稿表演；

⑤选取或布置适合本学习任务的场地进行本情景表演拍摄。

> 根据上述的介绍，请你完成如下的学习任务：

❶ 记录小组接待客户拜访任务的要点：

The team:	Name of product:
Detailed information	1. 2. 3.
I suggest	
I think	
I learn	

备注：欢迎大家登录课程的在线平台，点击观看往届学生的任务展示及教师点评。

扫一扫

2.4.3 模拟客户接待的即兴任务

在这个任务中，教师会扮演来你们公司拜访的客人，其在公司拜访期间可能会向相关人员了解这些信息（例如 its history、main/latest products、markets、employees、certificates、production capacity）等。同时，除了公司信息表上的信息外，他/她也会了解其他内容。因此，各位同学在课前要思考和准备上述信息、撰写必要的书面资料，并能在任务中做出及时、到位的应答。

> 根据上述的介绍，请你完成如下的学习任务：

❶ 团队根据分配到的任务编号学习相关的企业信息单。

❷ 团队分配任务，搜集该企业相关的文字和图片资料，并就客户拜访做积极准备。

❸ 在即兴任务进行时，请在同伴小组的任务单下记录相关的信息并做必要的评价。

› 即兴任务附件

No.1

Name	Taizhou Sunshine Furniture Co., Ltd.
Year of establishment	1999
Main products	Hotel bedroom furniture and its side ranges like doors, sofas, chairs, lobby furniture, restaurant furniture, office furniture and outdoor furniture, etc.
Latest product	Bedroom Nightstand(床头柜) • Style: Modern • Layer: 4 Layers • Model No.: ZRM-001 • Material: Wood •
Main markets	…
Export turnover	US$ 3, 000, 000
Production capacity	10, 000 PCS/month
Certificates	ISO9001, ISO14001, RoHS, CE
Employees	110
Nearest port(s)	

No.2

Name	JIAXING New-Star Leather Co., Ltd
Year of establishment	2001
Main products	Lady handbag, backpack, wallet, bag, fashion bag, hand-bag, messenger bag.
Latest product	Lady Handbag(女士手提包) • Style No. : Fashion • Specification: L28*H37*W10 cm • Material: PU •
Main markets	…
Export turnover	US$ 4, 000, 000
Production capacity	240, 000 PCS/year
Certificates	ISO9001, ISO14001, BSCI
Employees	200
Nearest port(s)	

No.3

Name	Wenzhou Zhicheng Optical Co., Ltd.
Year of establishment	2005
Main products	Eyeglasses, optical frames, sunglasses, glasses, eyewear frame, reading glasses, kid glasses.
Latest product	Women Sunglasses(女士太阳眼镜) ● Style: classical ● Color: grey ● Model No.: LATTE–S ● Material of frame: stainless steel ● Lenses: polarized lenses ●
Main markets	…
Export turnover	US$ 2, 000, 600
Production capacity	50, 000 PCS/year
Certificates	CE, FDA, UL, ISO9000
Employees	150
Nearest port(s)	

No.4

Name	Yiwu Arts & Crafts Co., Ltd.
Year of establishment	2000
Main products	Stuffed toys, plush toys, Teddy Bear, cushion, soft toys, promotional gifts, original toy, promotional items, and dinosaur gift.
Latest product	Valentine Hippo(情人节河马) ● Size:5–12 inches ● Age:Under 3 years ● Model No.:Hippo2–1 ● Material: plush ●
Main markets	…
Export turnover	US$ 3, 050, 000
Production capacity	5, 000, 000, 000 PCS/year
Certificates	Wal-Mart, Dollar General, BV, BSCI audit
Employees	100
Nearest port(s)	

No.5

Name	Ningbo Tenta Stationery Factory
Year of establishment	1998
Main products	Ball pen, leather pen, carbon fiber pen, plastic pen, metal pen, wood pen, paper pen, fountain pen.
Latest product	Ball Point Pen(圆珠笔) ● Color: black/blue ● Ink: 0.7 mm or 1.0 mm ● Model No.: A314 ● Material: metal
Main markets	…
Export turnover	US$ 1, 060, 500
Production capacity	8, 000, 000 PCS/month
Certificates	ISO 9001, Sedex
Employees	500
Nearest port(s)	

No.6

Name	Jinhua Evergreen Appliance Co., Ltd.
Year of establishment	2000
Main products	Water bottle pump, electric kettle, electric teapot, household meat grinder.
Latest product	Electric Kettle（电热水壶） ● Capacity: 2.0 L ● Volts: 220 V ● Model No.:1820 ● Material: stainless steel ●
Main markets	…
Export turnover	US$ 10, 503, 000
Production capacity	10, 000 PCS/month
Certificates	CE, CB
Employees	300
Nearest port(s)	

项目3 沟通价格

学习目标

知识目标

1. 了解产品报价的基本要求；
2. 理解价格条款沟通的要点和难点；
3. 掌握价格条款的英语表述和沟通策略。

能力目标

1. 能够根据价格磋商的主题搜集相关的资料；
2. 掌握如何同目标国客户就价格进行有效沟通；
3. 明确价格磋商任务要点并完成情景模拟任务。

任务 3.1 认识出口产品报价

扫一扫

在国际市场激烈的竞争中，价格优势往往是抢占国际市场份额的利器。面对客户询价，如何有效报价往往是摆在我们外贸新人面前的一个难题。首先，我们要了解产品在国际市场上的价格竞争现状；其次我们要尽可能采集客户及订单信息，在此基础上才能真正做到合理报价。换言之，面对不同的竞争对手、不同的客户及订单情况，我们给出的报价一定是不一样的。同时，我们也要转变观念：价格是重要优势，但不是唯一的优势。

> 根据上述的介绍，请你完成如下的学习任务：

❶ 分析价格优势：

相对竞争优势	绝对竞争优势

❷ 归纳影响客户下单的因素：

❸ 总结报价前需采集的客户信息：

1.

2.

3.

❹ 分析合理报价的策略：

类型	报价策略
试订单	
仅询价	

任务 3.2 分析价格沟通案例

扫一扫

3.2.1 介绍案例产品：出口 3D 墙板

越来越多的年轻人开始接受“轻装修、重装饰”的理念，3D 墙板已成为当前国内外建筑墙壁新潮的装饰产品，国际市场举起了一轮 3D 墙板的出口热潮。3D 墙板作为一种新型的装饰材料，应用了航天航空科技成果，采用不同的创新材质，环保性能好，视觉冲击强，满足了国际市场对装修材料的新需求和新要求。

> 根据上述的介绍，请你完成如下的学习任务：

❶ 列举制作工序：

❷ 罗列技术、工艺：

❸ 归纳产品优势：

1.

2.

3.

……

❹ 分析案例企业保持竞争力的方法：

扫一扫

3.2.2 价格沟通案例

【案例背景介绍】

浙江海宁的一家专业生产3D墙纸的企业接待了来自印度的新客户。Koala是公司资深的业务员，公司安排她负责接待来公司洽谈的客户Vijay。Vijay参观工厂后对企业的技术、生产和管理总体比较满意。双方在研发部就一款新产品价格展开洽谈。下面我们一起来学习如何议价。

Koala: Vijay, I have showed you around our factory. Now this is our R&D Department. You can learn more about our new products and take a break there.

Vijay: Thank you.

Koala: Coffee or black tea?

Vijay: Just black tea please.

Koala: OK. Zoe, black tea please.

Zoe: This is black tea for you.

Vijay: Thank you.

Vijay: It's very nice of you.

Koala: This is our latest catalogue.

...

Koala: Tell me your size and quantity please.

Vijay: It's 40 cm*40 cm. I want to order 6, 000 PCS, so it is for 20 GP.

Koala: It's $ 3.2/PC FOB Shanghai.

Vijay: Cheaper, please.

Koala: I think our price is very reasonable.

Vijay: No, no. It's too high for us to accept. Other suppliers' are much cheaper than yours.

Koala: Yes, but ours are better than theirs. As you can see, we use eco-friendly material. It is good at fireproof, heat insulation, moisture-proof, and sound-absorbing. And the product lifetime is 25–30 years. Look, the design and color are very beautiful.

Vijay: But my friend in India told me that this model was only $2.8/PC FOB Shanghai last year.

Koala: It was true. But as you know, cost of raw materials has been rising very quickly this year. And so has the labor cost. I'm sorry.

Vijay: I understand, but please give me some discount. I would like to do more business with you.

Koala: It is our rock bottom price this year. If you place a bigger order this time, a discount is considerable.

Vijay: 22, 000 PCS. It is for 40 HQ. And we will place more next time.

Koala: OK. Then how much discount do you ask for?

Vijay: 10% discount.

Koala: Sorry, I can only give you 5% discount.

Vijay: $2.9/PC, please.

Koala: No profit at this price. But I have to make a concession. So more orders in the future.

Vijay: All right, let's call it a deal.

Koala: Well, I have to admit that this price is only for our old clients. Let's keep our long-term cooperation in the future.

Vijay: Yes, of course.

Koala: Enjoy some fruits and if there is anything you want to know about this wall panel or other models, please let me know.

Vijay: Thank you.

> 根据上述的案例，请你完成如下的学习任务：

❶ 请把加框的单词填入表格并注上中文，并把画线的句子翻译在原文处。

1.	2.	3.	4.
5.	6.	7.	8.

❷ 重点跟读加框的单词、画线的句子并能准确、流利地读出来、说出来。

扫一扫

3.2.3 理解价格沟通案例

买家和卖家在出口订单的磋商中都会关注价格。价格磋商的要点是交换买卖双方的意见，找到双方都能接受的价格范围。一般而言，我们在国际展会、在线询单以及工厂参观后都可能涉及价格的磋商。

在本次的课程里，我们以案例企业新客人到工厂参观后的价格磋商为例和大家分享如何同客人谈价格。如何同我们的新客人谈价格呢？请大家跟随我们的课程一起进入今天的学习。

> 根据上述的介绍，请你完成如下的学习任务：

❶ 总结产品报价参考信息：

❷ 概括 Vijay 的砍价理由：

❸ 评价 Koala 就印度客人砍价的应对：

❹ 谈谈案例在商务礼仪方面给予你的启发：

扫一扫

3.2.4 分析印度市场及客户

印度是世界四大文明古国之一，早在公元前2000年就创造了灿烂的印度河文明。近年来，印度一跃成为世界上发展最快的国家之一，经济增长速度引人瞩目。我们一提到印度，就会联想到宝莱坞电影、印度歌舞、印度美食、遍布各地的美丽庙宇等等。印度这个人口众多、市场体量巨大的发展中国家在我国外贸出口中占有重要的一席之地。

> 根据上述的介绍，请你完成如下的学习任务：

❶ 列举印度的概况：

❷ 分析印度市场特点：

❸ 分析印度客户特点：

❹ 谈谈本视频对你的启发：

❺ 补充印度市场及客户分析：

任务3.3 分析议价拓展案例

扫一扫

我们在订单的谈判中常常遭遇客人的砍价。2009年6月，Cindy从学校毕业并进入了嘉兴当地一家生产真丝产品的企业，主要负责公司的蚕丝被出口业务。她经手的订单是在2009年1月出口到美国，而且余款已经结算完毕，但客户以该公司还向美国的其他买家出口了同类产品影响其销售，要求降价20%。为什么会遭遇这样的砍价呢？希望这则小案例能带给大家一些启发和思考。

> 根据上述的介绍，请你完成如下的学习任务：

❶ 分析蚕丝被的优点、出口市场：

❷ 分析客户售后砍价的原因：

客户本人的理由	
公司老板的分析	

❸ 总结Cindy对客户砍价的处理：

❹ 谈谈拓展案例给予你的启发：

任务3.4 模拟价格沟通任务

扫一扫

3.4.1 模拟产品报价任务

同学们，在对外报价中总会遇到客人砍价，我们要学会合理地陈述我方的报价。这样，才能维护我方的利益，也能使得客人更加认可我们的产品和报价。那么如何陈述呢？

首先，要根据客户的订单量报价，具体要明确是FOB、CIF，还是CFR以及其他贸易术语报价。

其次，在产品报价之后，要把影响价格的因素，如

①材料（material）

②款式（pattern）

③特别的技术或工艺（technique）

④销路（selling）

⑤成本的变化（cost）等进行陈述，说明价格的合理性。

【参考例文】

Justify My Price

Good morning, ladies and gentlemen. I'm Lucy from Zhejiang Rainbow Textile Co., Ltd.

Our offer comes as follows: 5,000 pieces of hand-embroidered silk scarves at USD25 per piece, CIF Hamburg.

My price is reasonable for the marketplace. First of all, we use 100% silk satin. Second, its design of geometry is quite in fashion and you can see our great workmanship from its edge hemming—hand rolling. Besides, the technique of Screen Printing is adopted. Besides, our workmanship and design are better than our competitors. I have to say that the costs of labor and raw materials keep rising in China. As you know this batch of products will be well received in your market. Therefore, our price is reasonable.

I will try my best to lower the price, but my quotation is the rock bottom price for the old friends. If you can place a large order, we might give you some discount.

Thanks for your attention. Any questions?

> 根据上述的介绍，请你完成如下的学习任务：

记录同学有关产品报价的汇报要点：

Reporter:	Name of product:
Detailed information	1. 2. 3.
I suggest	
I ask	
I learn	

备注：欢迎大家登录课程的在线平台，点击观看往届学生的任务展示及教师点评。

扫一扫

3.4.2　模拟同客户在其来公司拜访后议价的任务

在本学习任务中，每个分配到任务的学习小组将根据课程的学习，模拟同客户在其来公司/工厂拜访后在样品间议价。要求具体如下：

①双方在议价过程中要结合具体的产品以及订单量；在整个过程中，要有报价、砍价、各自陈述理由，并能最终达成双方都能接受的价格。

②准备相关资料，比如报价单、目录册、样品，有些材料也可以通过手提电脑来展示。

③出口商佩戴工作证、双方请穿着正装出镜。

④请在任务中脱稿表演。

⑤选取或布置适合本学习任务的场地进行情景表演拍摄。

> 根据上述的介绍，请你完成如下的学习任务：

记录有关小组议价任务的要点：

The team:	Name of product:
Detailed information	1. 2. 3.
I suggest	
I think	
I learn	

备注：欢迎大家登录课程的在线平台，点击观看往届学生的任务展示及教师点评。

扫一扫

3.4.3 模拟沟通价格的即兴任务

这个任务模拟客户与我方谈判价格的工作任务。重点请关注即兴任务的要点：双方之前有过合作，而本次是一个续订单。卖家要了解续订单的情况并给出一定的妥协，但是妥协要考虑到成本情况，也要考虑彼此长期的合作。我们在同客人就价格的沟通中也要把自身的品质、货期、服务等优势体现出来。扮演客户的A组要根据订单提出新的报价，并和对方进行协商；扮演卖家的B组要根据客人的新报价做出合理的应对，有礼有节地和对方进行协商。

> 根据上述的介绍，请你完成如下的学习任务：

❶ 团队根据分配到的任务编号学习相关的企业信息单。

❷ 团队分配任务，搜集该订单相关的文字和图片资料并就议价做积极的准备。

❸ 在即兴任务进行时，请在同伴小组的任务单下记录相关的信息并做必要的评价。

> 即兴任务附件

No.1

Team A (the buyer)

Product	**Kids Scooter**
Quantity	8, 000 PCS
Quotation	
Time of delivery	20th, Sept., 20___
The reduction you want	
The reduction you get	
The reasons for reduction	

Team B (the seller)

Product	**Kids Scooter**
Quantity	
Quotation	USD10–15/PC FOB Ningbo
Time of delivery	
The discount offered first	
Concessions	

No.2

Team A (the buyer)

Product	Metal Letter Shelf
Quantity	500, 000 PCS
Quotation	
Time of delivery	10th, Oct., 20___
The reduction you want	
The reduction you get	
The reasons for reduction	

Team B (the seller)

Product	Metal Letter Shelf
Quantity	
Quotation	USD1–1.5/PC FOB Shanghai
Time of delivery	
The discount offered first	
Concessions	

No.3

Team A (the buyer)

Product	**Children's Coat**
Quantity	1, 000 PCS
Quotation	
Time of delivery	20th, Jan., 20___
The reduction you want	
The reduction you get	
The reasons for reduction	

Team B (the seller)

Product	**Children's Coat**
Quantity	
Quotation	USD15–18/PC FOB Ningbo
Time of delivery	
The discount offered first	
Concessions	

No.4

Team A (the buyer)

Product	Wireless Pointer Presenter
Quantity	12, 000 PCS
Quotation	
Time of delivery	Within 1 month
The reduction you want	
The reduction you get	
The reasons for reduction	

Team B (the seller)

Product	Wireless Pointer Presenter
Quantity	
Quotation	USD12–14/PC FOB Qingdao
Time of delivery	
The discount offered first	
Concessions	

No.5

Team A (the buyer)

Product	Vacuum Lunch Box
Quantity	20, 000 PCS
Quotation	
Time of delivery	30th, May., 20___
The reduction you want	
The reduction you get	
The reasons for reduction	

Team B (the seller)

Product	Vacuum Lunch Box
Quantity	
Quotation	USD8–10/PC FOB Shanghai
Time of delivery	
The discount offered first	
Concessions	

No.6

Team A (the buyer)

Product	PVC Tablecloth
Quantity	1, 200 PCS
Quotation	
Time of delivery	Within 2 weeks
The reduction you want	
The reduction you get	
The reasons for reduction	

Team B (the seller)

Product	PVC Tablecloth
Quantity	
Quotation	USD12–15/meter FOB Shenzhen
Time of delivery	
The discount offered first	
Concessions	

项目 4 商务用餐

学习目标

知识目标

1. 了解涉外商务用餐的特点；
2. 理解涉外商务用餐的要点和难点；
3. 掌握涉外商务用餐的英语表述和沟通策略。

能力目标

1. 能够根据商务用餐的主题搜集相关的资料；
2. 掌握如何向目标国客户推荐合适的本地特色菜并做介绍；
3. 能够明确商务用餐的要点并完成情景模拟任务。

任务 4.1 认识商务用餐

扫一扫

在商务交往中，商务用餐可以营造轻松、融洽的氛围，也可以通过邀请品尝美味的食物、放松的交谈等活动拉近彼此的心理距离。因此，商务用餐虽是外贸人工作中的很小的一部分，但其作用和价值也要引起我们的重视。尽管不同的文化对于商务用餐在交往中的定位存在差异，但是我们都希望通过商务用餐表达对客户的尊重、重视和善意，为彼此增进商务沟通创设机会。

> 根据上述的介绍，请你完成如下的学习任务：

❶ 分析文化对生意关系的影响：

人情关系的文化	契约关系的文化

❷ 归纳商务用餐的定位：

❸ 总结商务用餐的注意点：

1.

2.

3.

❹ 谈谈如何获取客户的饮食信息：

任务 4.2 分析商务用餐的沟通案例

扫一扫

4.2.1 介绍案例产品：出口筷子

筷子是我们国家常用的饮食工具。朝鲜、韩国、日本、越南、泰国、蒙古国等亚洲国家的人民深受中国文化的影响，也会使用筷子进餐，而且在受华人文化影响的国家和地区的人民也会使用筷子。虽然一双筷子看似简单，但是各个目标国也会因饮食、法律等差异对材质、制作、处理等有不同的要求和标准。目前，我国的筷子产地主要集中在广东、浙江、福建、上海、山东、湖南、江苏等省市。

> 根据上述的介绍，请你完成如下的学习任务：

❶ 列举筷子的材质：

❷ 归纳木质、竹质筷子出口前的处理：

❸ 比较三国筷子的差异及原因：

种类	特点及原因
日本的筷子	
韩国的筷子	
中国的筷子	

❹ 总结我国一次性筷子的出口优势：

4.2.2 商务用餐沟通案例

扫一扫

【案例背景介绍】

杭州的一家专业生产筷子的企业接待了来自日本的客户。其中，Susan 是主要负责跟进的业务员，双方在工厂参观、合同洽谈等方面进展顺利。晚上，Susan 根据公司惯例宴请日本客人外出用餐，意在增进双方的了解和友谊。

Susan: Ok. We'll sit here. Take a seat，please.

Mr. Sakai: Thanks.

Waitress: Would you like some tea?

Mr. Sakai: Yes，please.

Waitress: Would you like some tea?

Susan: Yes，please. Thank you.

Susan: Today，we'll have dishes of typical Hangzhou style. What's your favorite food?

Mr. Sakai: Green vegetables and bean curd.

Susan: Is there anything that you don't eat?

Mr. Sakai: No animal innards, please.

Susan: Would you like noodles or local dim sums?

Mr. Sakai: Noodles please.

Susan: Ok. How about Sister Song's fish broth, noodles, bean curd, mushrooms, stir-fried cabbages with green and red peppers?

Mr. Sakai: Great! I like them, thank you.

Susan: What would you like to drink?

Mr. Sakai: Beer, please.

Susan: OK. 2 bottles of beer.

Waitress: Your dish please.

Mr. Sakai: Oh, Why do you call this dish "Sister Song's fish broth"?

Susan: In the Song Dynasty, there was a Sister Song. One day, her brother-in-law had a heavy cold. Sister Song cooked a broth with fish slices from the West Lake, ginger, scallion, vinegar sauce and bamboo shoots. He enjoyed the dish and soon recovered. Later on, the emperor also tasted her broth, which made her restaurant boom.

Mr. Sakai: It's so interesting. What do you usually do on weekends?

Susan: I will play badminton, eat out or go shopping with my friends. What about you?

Mr. Sakai: I always go sea fishing with family and friends.

Susan: It sounds fantastic! Please help yourself to the dishes and feel at home.

Mr. Sakai: Yes, of course, I'll. It's really to my taste. They all taste delicious.

Susan: Here! Let me propose a toast to our cooperation.

Mr. Sakai: I propose a toast to good health of your family and the successful conclusion of our negotiation. Cheers!

Susan: Cheers!

Mr. Sakai: Thank you very much. I'd like to thank you for your hospitality since our arrival in Hangzhou.

Susan: It's my pleasure.

Mr. Sakai: Here are small Japanese gifts for you.

Susan: You are so nice, and I like Japanese cookies very much. Thank you for cooperating with us. I will follow up your order carefully and please let us know if there is anything you need.

Mr. Sakai: Let's keep in contact. Thanks for this dinner.

Susan: Yes. Thank you for coming and sharing time with me.

> 根据上述的案例，请你完成如下的学习任务：

❶ 请把加框的单词填入表格并注上中文，并把画线的句子翻译在原文处。

1.	2.	3.	4.
5.	6.	7.	8.

❷ 重点跟读加框的单词、画线的句子并能准确、流利地读出来、说出来。

4.2.3 理解商务用餐沟通案例

有些客人来中国的时候可能行程非常满，没有时间坐下来用餐。但是，有些客人远道而来，在公司拜访和逗留的时间相对较长。在这种情况下，我们非常有必要宴请他们：首先，这是最基本的商务礼节；其次，客人可能对当地餐馆一点都不熟悉；此外，一起用餐可以让双方放松下来，增进彼此的了解和感情。我们如何同客人融洽、得体地用餐呢？请大家跟随我们的课程一起进入今天的学习内容。

> 根据上述的介绍，请你完成如下的学习任务：

❶ 分析点菜之前需了解的细节：

❷ 归纳“中国菜”介绍要点：

❸ 罗列Susan和客人用餐时的话题：

❹ 谈谈Susan营造用餐氛围的方法：

4.2.4 分析日本市场及客户

日本资源匮乏而且严重依赖进口，“二战”后经济迅速崛起，一跃成为世界经济强国、制造业强国。“精益求精”成为日本企业的代名词，比如一颗螺丝可以做二十年，长寿企业数量远远超过了世界其他国家。作为岛国，日本的海上交通便捷，大大便利其发展对外贸易。近年来，中日两国的双边贸易规模不断扩大，互为重要的贸易合作伙伴。日本融合了东西方文明，散发着浓郁的现代与传统气息，不断书写地理小国的经济强国传奇。

> 根据上述的介绍，请你完成如下的学习任务：

❶ 罗列日本的概况：

❷ 分析日本市场特点：

❸ 分析日本客户特点：

❹ 谈谈本视频给予你的启发：

❺ 补充日本市场及客户分析：

任务 4.3 分析商务用餐拓展案例

扫一扫

客户到公司拜访重在谈生意，但是如果客户有意向或是明确提出在中国当地逗留或是游玩，我们就应该抓住增进彼此友谊、加深了解的绝佳机会。Tom 毕业后不久在嘉兴当地的外贸企业工作，当时他负责公司的太阳能产品出口业务。这个案例发生在他进入公司的第二年。公司对大学毕业的 Tom 非常信任，安排他负责全程接待来自丹麦的客人 John。John 是通过展会认识了这家企业并决定亲自来中国，也希望深度体验一下当地的风土人情。希望这则小案例能带给大家一些启发和思考。

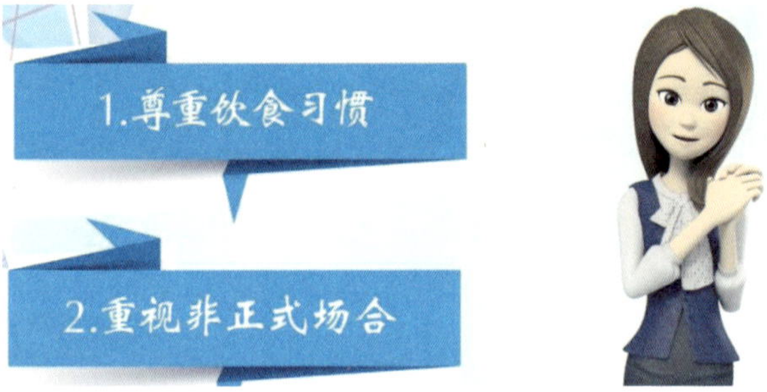

> 根据上述的介绍，请你完成如下的学习任务：

❶ 分析 Tom 的客户接待情况：

片段 1	
片段 2	

❷ 归纳接待客户的注意点：

❸ 概括客户商务用餐的情景及作用：

片段	情景	作用
片段1		
片段2		
片段3		

❹ 谈谈拓展案例给予你的启发：

任务 4.4 模拟商务用餐等沟通任务

扫一扫

4.4.1 模拟介绍一道中国菜的任务

同学们，我们招待客户用餐时有必要对中国菜做简要的介绍。一般而言，客人一般想知道食材和烹饪法，因此通过本次学习希望我们今后能在点菜、用餐时向客人做必要的介绍和说明。首先，请翻译选中的中国菜。其实，网站有很多现成的菜名，大家可以根据如下菜谱翻译法选取合适的菜名。菜谱翻译的方法主要如下：（1）直译法。即译出或表达出原词、原句、原文的字面意思且忠实于原作的翻译方法。采用这种方法进行翻译时可以根据公式进行翻译。具体如下：

烹调法＋刀法＋A (with/and) B ＋ in/with ＋(garlic/soy/brown/spicy) sauce

①按照上面的结构进行翻译时，烹调法和刀法常用过去分词形式。

②A和B均代表菜的原料。

③如果原料A为主料，B为辅料，则使用with作连词；如果原料A和原料B基本等量，则使用and作连词。

比如：北京烤鸭——Beijing roasted duck。

龙井虾仁——shelled shrimps with Dragon Well tea。

鱼香肉丝——shredded pork in garlic sauce。

（2）菜谱意译法。由于中国饮食文化源远流长，很多菜名有丰富的文化色彩，因此为了便于西方人理解和明白，不拘泥于原文形式的译法，也就是在翻译的过程中还原这道菜的烹调法、刀法、原料等。

比如：翡翠虾仁——shelled shrimps with green vegetables。

凤凰投林——stir-fried chicken shreds with Chinese chive。

其次，简要介绍这道菜的做法。希望能图文并茂，条理清楚，步骤明确，并在可能的情况下简要引入这道菜的历史典故。

【参考例文】

A Local Dish to My Client from Singapore

Good morning, ladies and gentlemen, I'm Sandy. I would like to introduce this dish to my client, a Singaporean Chinese. It is called Dongpo pork, a famous Chinese dish.

Dongpo pork is quite good in color, smell and taste. So it is favored greatly by people. Its cooking is quite easy but takes long time. First cut the streaky pork into large pieces, put shallot and ginger into the pot, add wine, sugar, soy sauce and water and then stew it on a slow fire for over an hour. When the pork is drying up, just add some wine during stewing.

It is said that this dish was created some 900 years ago in Hangzhou by Chinese poet Su Dongpo. During his term in Hang Zhou, he undertook various waterworks such as clearing waters of the Westlake and building of bridges. Therefore local people gave him the pork as gifts. And he loved cooking and cooked the pork in a unique way. And his cooking was passed down since then. And I believe that my client will enjoy this special dish.

Thanks for your attention, Any questions?

> 根据上述的介绍，请你完成如下的学习任务：

记录同学有关中国菜汇报要点：

Reporter:	Name of dish:
Detailed information	1. 2. 3.
I suggest	
I ask	
I learn	

备注：欢迎大家登录课程的在线平台，点击观看往届学生的任务展示及教师点评。

扫一扫

4.4.2 模拟陪同来访客户用餐的任务

在这个学习任务中，每个分配到任务的学习小组将根据课程的学习，模拟在公司/工厂拜访结束后，一起外出用餐。要求具体如下：

①巧妙设置表演情景。建议可以实地拍摄，也可以创设类似的环境。

②准备相关资料，比如菜单，也可以用电子菜单。

③在内容设计上要注意：点菜及点酒水要符合目标国市场客户的饮食及文化特点；适当地介绍中国菜的信息；交流客户拜访中涉及的部分信息；活跃用餐氛围，比如敬酒等。

④请正装出镜，请在任务中脱稿表演；展现恰当的餐桌礼仪，比如主动为客人调整座位，避免为客人夹菜，但可以增设公用餐具；了解客人是否会用筷子（chopsticks）；等等。

> 根据上述的介绍，请你完成如下的学习任务：

记录有关小组陪同客户用餐任务要点：

The team:	Name of dish:
Detailed information	1. 2. 3.
I suggest	
I think	
I learn	

备注：欢迎大家登录课程的在线平台，点击观看往届学生的任务展示及教师点评。

扫一扫

4.4.3 模拟商务接待的即兴任务

在这个任务中，模拟为客户安排当地一日游的行程。行程安排的重点主要包括：旅游（doing sightseeing）、购物（going shopping）、品尝当地特色美食（taking local food）。安排这些活动重在增进双方的感情和了解，行程安排要符合所在城市实际情况、客人的时间表，尊重和考虑客人的饮食习惯。在本即兴表演中，教师会扮演客人并向你们沟通了解为期一天行程的具体安排。各位同学在课前充分讨论和准备你们团队有关行程的安排，积极为客人做精心的设计。

> 根据上述的介绍，请你完成如下的学习任务：

❶ 团队根据分配到的任务编号学习相关的客户接待的信息单。

❷ 团队分配任务，根据所在城市及客户情况搜集相关的文字和图片资料并完成行程安排。

Schedule

Time	Activities
9:00–11:00	1.
	2.
	3.
11:00–13:30	1.
	2.
	3.
13:30–16:00	1.
	2.
	3.
16:00–18:30	1.
	2.

❸ 在即兴任务进行时，请在同伴小组的任务单下记录相关的信息并做必要的评价。

> 即兴任务附件

No.1

9月初，英国的老客户前往宁波当地的一家生产企业拜访。双方多年来合作非常顺利。宁波的企业计划邀请客人在当地游玩、叙旧，英国的客人欣然答应。请你为企业精心策划一日的行程。

Some suggestions:

—**Tianyi Square**: the oldest private library extant in China which has been made one of the key national heritage sites

—**The Drum Tower**: the only city tower of Ningbo

—**The Moon Lake**: "West Lake" of locals

—**Old Chenghuang Temple**: the newly-built shopping mall inheriting the Ming and Qing Dynasties' architectural style of the old temple

…

No.2

10月初，瑞典的老客户前往绍兴当地的一家服装企业拜访。双方多年来合作非常愉快。绍兴的企业计划邀请客人在当地游玩、叙旧，瑞典的客户表示同意。请你精心策划一日的行程。

Some suggestions:

—**Shen's Garden:** This garden boasts more than 800 years of history. In Song Dynasty, Poet Lu You fell in love in Tang Wan in this very garden, and composed a poem on the wall in the garden. They were separated by their parents from both sides.

—**Lan Pavilion:** During the Spring and Autumn Period, the king of Yue planted orchids here and later a pavilion was constructed here during the Han Dynasty. In 353 A.D., the noted calligrapher Wang Xizhi wrote some of his celebrated calligraphy here. Since then, the Orchid Pavilion has been known as a home of Calligraphy.

—**East Lake:** Located at the eastern suburbs of Shaoxing, East Lake is an elegant scenic spot comprising lakes, mountains and stone cliff structures. What's truly unique about East Lake is the three fascinating caves. Taking a traditional Wupeng boat tour on East Lake is the best way to take in its magnificent scenery and to experience its spectacular caves.

No.3

8月底，日本的新客户前往温州当地的一家生产企业拜访。双方谈判进展顺利，签下了大订单。企业计划邀请客人在当地逗留、游玩，日本的客人欣然答应。请你精心策划两日游的行程。

Some suggestions:

—**Jiangxin Island:** An island in the middle of the Oujiang river that runs through Wenzhou. The island has an old pagoda and a new pagoda, large areas of garden and lakes, a water park and a theme park. The theme park is known for its Ferris wheel which gives great views of both sides of the river and also a death-defying roller coaster.

—**Yandang Mountain:** it is 1,150 meters high. In Chinese, Yandang means "reed marsh for wild geese". In autumn, wild geese do gather in the marshes around the lake at the top of the mountain. It is famous for its peaks, waterfalls, and rocks.

—**Nanxi River Scenic Area:** The whole scenic area covers a land of 671 square kilometers, staging over 800 tourist sites in eight main scenic spots renowned for charming water, grotesque rocks, tremendous waterfalls, antique villages, and elegant forests.

No.4

11月初，埃及的新客户前往嘉兴当地的一家生产企业拜访。双方谈判进展顺利，客人计划在当地游玩、购物一天，希望嘉兴的企业为其制订行程，而企业方面也很有意向通过此次一日游增进双方的感情。

Some suggestions:

—**WuZhen:** Wuzhen displays its 6000-year history through its ancient stone bridges, stone pathways and delicate wood carvings. People can visit Mao Dun Museum, see special Waterfront houses and bridges, and enjoy canals in its river. And Wuzhen is the permanent host place of the World Internet Conference since 2014.

—**Xitang Ancient Town:** Known as one of the top six ancient towns in southern China, the town has a gentle climate, floating rills, ancient bridges and maintains, and an overall slow-paced lifestyle. Inside the town, there are many well-preserved buildings and 27 ancient bridges in the Ming and Qing dynasties.

—**The Qiantang Tide**: Qiantang River is the biggest river in Zhejiang Province, running from the west to Hangzhou Bay in the east. The soaring tide of the Qiantang River is a marvelous spectacle and the water can rise up to a height of 30 feet. Yanguan in Haining city is the best place to watch the Qiantang Tide.

No.5

4月初，俄罗斯的老客户前往杭州当地的一家贸易公司谈新订单。双方一直以来合作愉快，这次签下一个大单。公司计划邀请客人在当地逗留、游玩，俄罗斯的客人欣然答应。请你精心策划一日游的行程。

Some suggestions:

—**West Lake Scenic Area**: It has been among the most important sources of inspiration for Chinese garden designers via the numerous temples (e.g., Lingyin Temple), pagodas (e.g., Leifeng Pagoda), gardens, and artificial islands within the lake.

—**Longjing Village**: Walking along the path, one's eyes will be filled with the lush green tea gardens, and the well-proportioned Longjing Village lying just at the foot of the mountain. The ending point of the route is China National Tea Museum, which is a tea culture experience park.

—**Xixi National Wetland Park**: It is the first and only national wetland park in china, which combines urban wetland, farming wetland and cultural wetland.

No.6

6月初，美国的大客户前往台州当地的一家生产企业考核企业并看新产品。双方一直以来合作愉快，企业计划邀请客人在当地逗留、游玩，美国的客人欣然答应。请你精心策划一日游的行程。

Some suggestions:

—**Linhai Ancient Great Wall**: it was built in the Eastern Jin Dynasty. This ancient wall used to be a stronghold against outside invasion and to protect the city from big floods. It boasts an unusual landscape, surrounded by green hills and fresh waters.

—**Tiantai Mountain**: Its highest peak, Huading, reaches a height of 1,138 meters. Guoqing Temple on the mountain is the headquarters of Tiantai Buddhism and also a tourist destination. There are Shiliang Waterfall viewed as a masterpiece of nature and Huading Peak which is the best place to view sunrise.

项目5 沟通品质

学习目标

知识目标

1. 了解产品品质的作用和价值；
2. 理解产品品质沟通的要点和难点；
3. 掌握产品品质英语表述和沟通策略。

能力目标

1. 能够根据产品品质的主题搜集相关的资料；
2. 能够同目标国客户就产品品质展开有效沟通；
3. 能够明确品质磋商要点并完成情景模拟沟通任务。

任务 5.1 认识出口产品品质

面对国际市场激烈的竞争，产品品质是不少中小企业提升出口竞争力的重要途径。欧美市场相对比较成熟，其产品的生产标准、检测标准等一般高于我们国内标准。在获取订单、抢占国际市场的过程中，我们的出口企业在品质方面迅速成长，近几年逐渐摆脱了单一的“低价竞争”。同时，我们也应该看到不同的出口市场对品质要求和需求存在着差异。

> 根据上述的介绍，请你完成如下的学习任务：

❶ 概括欧美市场对品质的要求：

❷ 分析品质与价格的关系：

❸ 总结提升品质同时控制成本的方法：

1.

2.

3.

……

❹ 归纳品质的要素组成：

使用性能	外观性能

其他性能：

任务 5.2 分析品质沟通案例

5.2.1 介绍案例产品：出口服装

中国是全球纺织产业规模最大的国家，同时也是产业链最为完整、门类最齐全的国家。其中，我国的纺织品主要包括纱线面料、服装等。近年来，尽管我国人口红利的优势不再，但是产业优势依然强大。目前，我国服装主要销往美国、欧盟、日本等传统市场，相关的企业也在不断打开和开发新兴市场。

> 根据上述的介绍，请你完成如下的学习任务：

❶ 分析面料特点：

梭织面料	
针织面料	

❷ 概括防止染料活移的方法：

种类	举例

概括俄罗斯辅料的特点：

❹ 确定出口服装版型的方法：

5.2.2 品质沟通案例

扫一扫

【案例背景介绍】

Cathy就职于一家贸易型的服装出口企业。她根据自己的从业经验和目标市场特点，带了一批样品前往俄罗斯大客户位于上海的办公室进行拜访。在短短1个小时的拜访期间，大客户会根据她的样品决定今年的订单量。双方在交流中重点涉及了样品的品质。双方就其中某一订单中查出的品质问题进行了沟通和解决。

Roman: Hi, Cathy.

Cathy: Hi, Roman. Nice to meet you again.

Roman: Me too.

Cathy: I have brought with me all the samples you're interested in.

Roman: Thanks.

Cathy: And I will show you our latest catalogue.

Roman: Ok. Now let's start.

Cathy: Yes, please tell me the style No. you are interested in.

Roman: Please show me Sample No.047002601.

Cathy: Yes, here it is.

Roman: I like this design. The material, the accessories, and the colors are really great.

Cathy: I'm very happy to hear that. So do you have any special requirements for quality?

Roman: Use silk threads for blind stitch. It's 2.5 cm wide.

Cathy: Do you mean the bottom and sleeve bottom?

Roman: Yeah.

Cathy: Yes, I see. We will pay attention to bulk production.

Roman: The washing shrinkage should be within 5% and no more please.

Cathy: Yes, I have got it.

Roman: Yes, that's right. As for color fastness, 3-4 is accepted. So much for this sample.

Cathy: Can you tell me your quantity?

Roman: 100, 000 PCS. Let's move on to the next one?

Cathy: Yes, of course.

...

Roman: Hello, Cathy. Can we discuss about some problems of bulk No.047002601.

Cathy: Yes, please.

Roman: It's the color. We find out that your color fastness is not up to 3-4 level according to the test.

Cathy: Oh, I'm so sorry that. You know the color of the yarns were beyond our control. Can you accept it if we change the washing care label to "DRY WASH"? The additional fees will be on us.

Roman: Ok, I think I have no better choice.

Cathy: Sorry.

Roman: Could you give us some discount?

Cathy: How much?

Roman: 3%.

Cathy: I can only offer 2%. Otherwise, we have no profits.

Roman: Ok. I accept.

Cathy: Thank you very much.

Roman: Ok, Bye!

Cathy: Have a good day. Bye!

> 根据上述的案例，请你完成如下的学习任务：

❶ 请把加框的单词填入表格并注上中文，并把画线的句子翻译在原文处。

1.	2.	3.	4.
5.	6.	7.	8.

❷ 重点跟读加框的单词、画线的句子并能准确、流利地读出来、说出来。

扫一扫

5.2.3 理解品质沟通案例

这个单元我们以大家比较熟悉的服装产品为例侧重学习如何同客人沟通和交流产品品质。在外贸订单的跟进过程中，品质一直是国际买家关注的要点。那么，在订单的开发中如何确切地了解客人的品质要求？在实际的生产中，如何通过有效的沟通解决产品的品质问题？请大家跟随我们的课程一起进入今天的学习内容。

> 根据上述的介绍，请你完成如下的学习任务：

❶ 分析客户Roman在订单沟通时对品质的要求：

1.

2.

3.

❷ 简述客户 Roman 在中查时发现的主要问题：

❸ 概括 Cathy 面对客人提出的品质问题的应对方法：

❹ 分析色差产生的原因及对策：

扫一扫

5.2.4 分析俄罗斯市场及客户

俄罗斯地跨欧亚两大洲，国土面积居世界首位，享有世界上最大的矿产储量，也是主要的石油和天然气出口国。俄罗斯经济基础雄厚，虽然近年来经济发展较为缓慢，但拥有巨大的经济潜力。中俄两国有着悠久的贸易往来历史，两国贸易的互补性强、合作基础良好。近年来，中俄两国的贸易关系不断升温，中国成为俄罗斯最大的贸易合作伙伴。

> 根据上述的介绍，请你完成如下的学习任务：

❶ 列举俄罗斯的概况：

❷ 分析俄罗斯市场特点：

❸ 分析俄罗斯客户特点：

❹ 谈谈本视频给你的启发：

❺ 补充俄罗斯市场及客户分析：

任务 5.3 分析品质沟通拓展案例

扫一扫

在对外贸易中，客人非常在意产品的品质。我们很多同学在中小外贸企业就职，往往同时承担谈订单、跟订单的工作任务。Wendy 毕业以来一直在家乡义乌从事各种小商品的出口业务，她接的订单虽然不大，但是客人下单频繁而且量多。她手上的这票 8, 000, 000PCS 纸杯预计 15 天后出口到法国，工期比较紧。面对产品无法“按质出口”，她在紧张的工期中如何应对？希望这则小案例能带给大家一些启发和思考。

> 根据上述的介绍，请你完成如下的学习任务：

❶ 分析产品出现的品质问题：

❷ 总结Wendy在生产工厂拒绝整改后可能的选择：

选择A	
选择B	
选择C	

❸ 评价Wendy的沟通策略：

❹ 谈谈案例给予你的启发：

任务5.4 模拟品质沟通任务

扫一扫

5.4.1 模拟介绍出口产品品质的任务

同学们，品质在对外贸易中发挥着重要的作用。首先，请确定相关的产品，不同的产品在质量表达的方法上有差异。比如，工业制成品的品质的介绍主要包括材质、性能、安全性、适用性、回收性等等；农产品则侧重于产地、等级、规格等。

其次，搜集和整合有关出口产品的品质的资料。比如，我们要介绍一款小家电，可以上相关企业的官网、http：//www.made-in-china.com、https：//www.alibaba.com等专业网站查阅中英文的产品品质信息，学习专业的英语表述方式。此外，根据产品特点，选择合适的汇报和呈现方式。

【参考例文】

A Quality Introduction to the Street LED Light

Good morning. Ladies and gentlemen. I'm Sandy. I would like to introduce the quality of the street LED light.

This street LED light, No. LD-35, is made of High-quality steel. Its light has long lifetime up to more than 50, 000–100,000 h. With unique design, this light covers the required lighting areas. Meanwhile, this illumination efficiency can save over 30% than similar products. Its average life is more than 8, 000 h. And designed with voltage device, it is safe to use in the public places.

In a word, it has a number of advantages of environmental protection, no pollution, less consumption, high efficiency, and long lifespan and so on. Besides, we have the certificates of CE, RoHS and FCC.

Thank You. Any questions?

> 根据上述的介绍，请你完成如下的学习任务：

记录同学有关品质汇报要点：

Reporter:	Name of product:
Detailed information	1. 2. 3.
I suggest	
I ask	
I learn	

备注：欢迎大家登录课程的在线平台，点击观看往届学生的任务展示及教师点评。

5.4.2 模拟同客户沟通品质的任务

扫一扫

在这个学习任务中，每个分配到任务的学习小组将根据课程的学习，模拟某一特定产品品质沟通的任务。任务的要求具体如下：

①设计、布置表演场景。同学们可以思考在什么情景下会向客人介绍产品的品质，按照这个思路创设表演场景。

②准备相关资料，比如样品、目录册。

③在品质介绍时要注意：介绍产品的性能、规格、材质、等级等等时，英语用词要专业、准确。另外，恰当地使用肢体语言来更好地支持你们的介绍。

④请正装出镜；请在任务中脱稿表演。

⑤在视频的后期制作中，对于涉及产品品质的专业词汇请在视频中以中英文字幕的形式出现，方便大家学习。

> 根据上述的介绍，请你完成如下的学习任务：

记录有关小组品质沟通任务要点：

The team:	Name of product:
Detailed information	1. 2. 3.
I suggest	
I think	
I learn	

备注：欢迎大家登录课程的在线平台，点击观看往届学生的任务展示及教师点评。

扫一扫

5.4.3 模拟沟通品质的即兴任务

在这个任务中，模拟与客户就品质展开进一步磋商。一般而言，品质是对外贸易中客户最为看重的一点。任务的要点是：卖家能把产品的品质介绍清楚；买家基于卖家的介绍要提出自己对品质的要求和建议。在即兴表演中，随机搭配的小组分别扮演客户和卖家，扮演客户的A组重在了解卖家的产品品质，并提出相应的品质要求。扮演卖家的B组在了解卖家的产品品质情况下，根据自己的市场要求提出相应的品质改进的要求。

> 根据上述的介绍，请你完成如下的学习任务：

❶ 团队根据分配到的任务编号学习相关的品质沟通的信息单。

❷ 团队分配任务，根据相关的产品品质信息搜集相关的文字和图片资料并完成准备工作。

❸ 在即兴任务进行前，请根据各自的任务完成表格的相关内容。

Team A (the buyer)

Product	
Country	
Quantity	
Time of delivery	
Information of quality	
Special requirements for quality	

Team B (the seller)

Product	
Country	
Minimum order quantity	
Time of delivery	
Quotation	
Key points of quality	
Improvements of quality for the client	

❹ 在即兴任务进行时，请在同伴小组的任务单下记录相关的信息并做必要的评价。

即兴任务附件

No.1 High Clear Rum Glass Bottle

Introduction：

A 10-year experience of making glass bottles

Main markets：Asia，USA，Europe and Africa

Unique design

Support on ODM&OEM

About product：

① Super flint(硬) glass

② The Customer's logo is accepted

③ Eco-friendly(环保) screen printing

④ A wide range of styles

⑤ Good service and competitive price

No.2 Photo Frame

Introduction：

13-year experience in manufacturing with a professional R&D team

Main markets：more than 500 clients over Europe，America and Asia

Support OEM&ODM

Certificates：...

About product：

① Glass and Metal

② Customized design is acceptable

③ More than 100 new styles every month

④ Best service and competitive price

No.3 Sofa

Introduction:

We have a 10-year experience of making sofa

Main markets: Europe, America, Japan, Korea, Southeast Asia and the Middle East

High-grade office furniture

Certificates: ...

Unique design

About product:

① 100% leather

② Customized color and design are welcome.

③ Competitive price, best quality, and best service

No.4 Multi-Function 7D Gaming Mouse

Introduction:

Making mouse and keyboard for over 7 years

Main markets: Europe, America, Australia, Asia, and the Middle East, etc.

Support on OEM/ODM orders

About product:

① Material: ABS

② 7D gaming mouse with the multi-media function

③ 1.5 m braided cable with a USB golden connector(连接器)

④ Soft touch rubber coating and comfortable hand feeling

⑤ Good at locating accurately and sensitively

No.5 Laptop Backpack

Introduction:

More than 10 years in this area

Main markets: America, Brazil, Mexico, Chile, and Columbia

Unique design

Support on ODM&OEM

About product:

① Customized logo and size are welcome

② Adjustable and comfortable shoulder

Straps & padded back panel

③ Available in different materials and

Assorted colors

No.6 Porcelain Cup

Introduction:

More than 10 years of making porcelain cup

Main market: Asia and USA

High quality

Unique design

Certificates:...

About product:

① High grade porcelain

② Customized logo, website, phone numbers or any of your ideas are welcome.

③ Heat Preservation

④ Health Care

⑤ Suitable for microwave and dishwasher

项目6 沟通包装

学习目标

知识目标

1. 了解产品内外包装的作用和价值；
2. 理解产品包装沟通的要点和难点；
3. 掌握产品包装英语表述和沟通策略。

能力目标

1. 能够根据产品内外包装的主题搜集相关的资料；
2. 能够同目标国客户就包装展开有效沟通；
3. 能够明确产品包装磋商要点并完成情景模拟任务。

任务6.1 认识出口产品包装

出口包装基本分为运输包装（即外包装）和销售包装（即内包装）。由于国际贸易运输线路长、气候差别大、装卸环节较多且与国内港口的设施及设备差异大，这就要求运输包装适应这些客观条件。此外，目标国的法律、文化、生活方式及水平、风俗习惯等各不相同，也会影响出口商品的销售包装。包装也是国际贸易中履约的一部分，因此要做到货物包装与行业习惯相符、符合进口商在合同中提出的包装要求。

> 根据上述的介绍，请你完成如下的学习任务：

❶ 概括包装不当的后果：

❷ 比较销售包装的种类：

陈列类	
识别类	
使用类	

分析销售包装的作用：

❸ 分析运输包装的种类：

箱	
袋	
包	
桶	

❹ 罗列运输包装印刷的主要信息：

任务6.2 分析包装沟通案例

扫一扫

6.2.1 介绍案例产品：出口婴儿衣物用品

婴儿用品也称为婴幼儿用品，是给0—3岁的婴儿群体提供的专业健康产品。由于婴幼儿特殊的体质、特殊的生理心理需求，一般进口国对婴儿用品在面料、染料、配件、设计等方面要求比较高，从而确保产品的安全性。

> 根据上述的介绍，请你完成如下的学习任务：

❶ 分析进口国对婴儿产品高要求的原因：

❷ 列举婴儿产品分类：

❸ 总结案例产品材质及特点：

❹ 分析婴儿产品出口要求：

化学指标	
辅件设计	

6.2.2 包装沟通案例

扫一扫

【案例背景介绍】

Ian就职于一家贸易型的出口企业，主要经营各类小商品。不久前，他接到了来自法国客人一票婴儿口水巾的订单。之前，客户已经找了多个卖家，但都因为货物包装没有达到其要求而没有谈成。下面我们一起来学习Ian如何跟进客户的包装要求并成功接到订单。

Ian: The bibs of your order will be 100% cotton, soft, AZO-free & eco-friendly. So can we discuss about packing now, Baptiste?

Baptiste: Yes, of course. And please tell me your packing.

Ian: As usual, one piece is packed in one OPP bag, and 500 pieces in a carton.

Baptiste: It's too simple. I'm afraid such packing cannot boost the sales.

Ian: How about OPP bags with card heads? You can choose up to 10 colors. This is the sample, and please take a look.

Baptiste: It's better. But it's far from what I want.

Ian: So what do you want, Baptiste?

Baptiste: Fine. My target customers are the middle-class in France. They will pay a lot of attention to the packing. So I want you to change in this way: one piece to be packed in an OPP bag; pink, blue and orange equally assorted in a gift box with a window. Wait for a moment, I will send you the picture.

Ian: I got it. Yeah, I can make the packing as you ask for. Do you have any requirement on the printing of gift box?

Baptiste: Please print the gift box with the cartoon donkey I send you now. It's quite popular with our kids.

Ian: Ok, I see. And mark the name of commodity and logo on the front of the box, and materials, colors, directions for washing, sizes, certificates and bar codes on the back of the box.

Baptiste: That's right. Please don't forget the recycle marks.

Ian: Oh, yes. I have added.

Baptiste: Great. How soon can I see the sample of packing?

Ian: Well, we will prepare the sample as per your instructions within 3 days. And as soon as I get the samples, I will contact you.

Baptiste: Thanks.

…

Ian: Hello, Baptiste Can I show you the samples of gift box now?

Baptiste: Yes, please.

Ian: We design three packing samples and I will send the pictures to you by WECHAT. Pleases check them out and reply to me.

Baptiste: Thank you very much. And wait for a moment. Well, I like the design of Picture 2 very much. This is exactly what I want. Well done.

Ian: I'm happy to hear that.

Baptiste: Please tell me the cost of the new packing.

Ian: It's 1 dollar per piece.

Baptiste: Ok, done!

> 根据上述的案例，请你完成如下的学习任务：

❶ 请把加框的单词填入表格并注上中文，并把画线的句子翻译在原文处。

1.	2.	3.	4.
5.	6.	7.	8.

❷ 重点跟读加框的单词、画线的句子并能准确、流利地读出来、说出来。

6.2.3 理解包装沟通案例

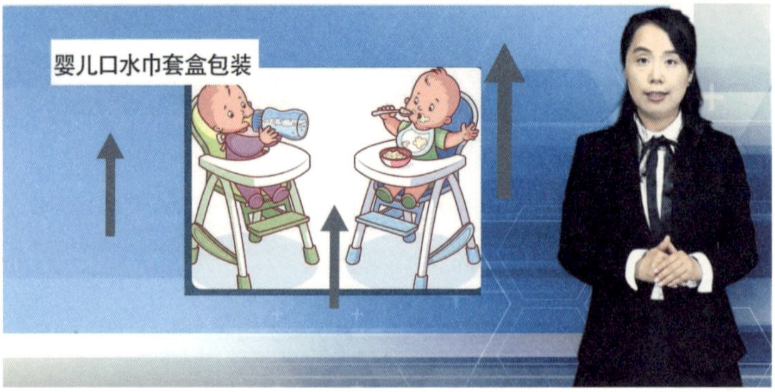

包装在出口中起到保护商品、促进销售的作用。很多国家，尤其是发达国家对进口产品的包装要求比较高，因此我们要和客人在前期订单的开发中积极沟通、跟进客人的包装需求。很多订单因为包装而提升了商品价值，也有不少订单因为包装不当而被拒收。如何确切地了解客人的包装要求，并让客人满意呢？请大家跟随我们的课程一起进入今天的学习。

> 根据上述的介绍，请你完成如下的学习任务：

❶ 解释“AZO-free”：

❷ 概括 Ian 公司口水巾常用的包装：

❸ 分析客人要求的礼盒印刷要求：

❹ 谈谈本案例给予你的启发：

6.2.4 分析法国市场及客户

扫一扫

法国位于欧洲西部、本土呈六边形，是西欧面积最大的国家。法国文化崇尚浪漫、自由，这是历经漫长的岁月逐渐沉淀并形成的一种生活态度。法国被誉为世界上最吸引人的浪漫国度。法国人天性率真、浪漫，热爱大自然。法国是发达国家之一，也是世界贸易大国。自中法两国建交以来双边经贸合作稳步发展，当下在“一带一路”推动下中法两国贸易的种类呈多样化发展。

> 根据上述的介绍，请你完成如下的学习任务：

❶ 罗列法国的概况：

❷ 分析法国市场特点：

❸ 分析法国客户特点：

❹ 谈谈本视频给你的启发：

❺ 补充法国市场及客户分析：

任务6.3 分析包装沟通拓展案例

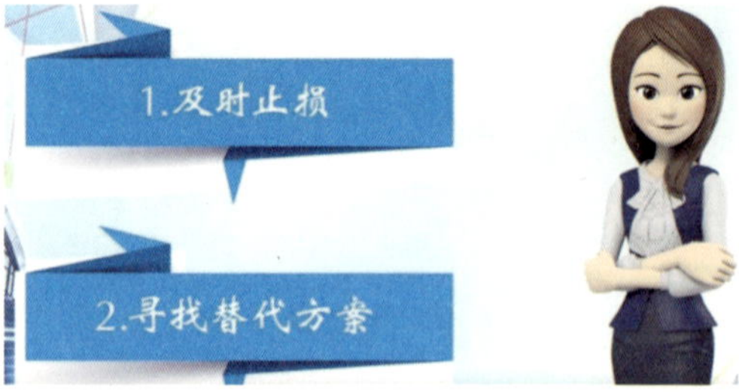

在外贸中，客人非常在意产品的品质。Charlie就职于杭州一家纺织品出口公司，他经手这一票10,000PCS用作促销品的空调被，原本计划在当年的6月出口到新加坡以推进空调的销售。他在装运前10天接到客人要求临时调整纸箱规格的紧急通知，货物还能顺利出口吗？希望这则小案例能带给大家对细节的启发和思考。

> 根据上述的介绍，请你完成如下的学习任务：

❶ 概括客户提出的包装更改要求：

1.	
2.	

❷ 评价厂家和Charlie都能接受的折中方案：

1.

2.

3.

❸ 分析货物被新加坡海关扣压的原因：

❹ 谈谈拓展案例给予你的启发：

任务6.4 模拟包装沟通任务

6.4.1 模拟介绍出口产品包装的任务

同学们，包装在对外贸易中发挥着不可忽视的作用。优良的包装可能会带来订单，包装不当也可能导致货物被拒收。这个任务是关于产品包装的介绍，主要包括产品的销售包装以及运输包装。

首先，包装同货物密切相关。请大家首先确定相关的产品并在汇报中明确说明产品。其次，根据你选取的产品搜集有关此类产品的包装资料。比如，我们要介绍一款出口到日本的绿茶，就要考虑到：①茶叶对包装的要求是防潮、防串味；②日本市场对茶叶销售包装、运输包装的要求；③运输方式。在搜集资料的过程中，同学们要充分利用我们专业的网站信息，也可以关注相关企业的中英文网站信息，学习专业的英语包装表述方式。

此外，根据产品特点，选择合适的汇报和呈现方式。比如，你手上有这个产品及其包装，就可以通过现场演示的方法汇报；如果你有比较多的图片信息，可以采用PPT来汇报。

【参考例文】

An Introduction to Packing Lemon Slicers

Good morning. Ladies and gentlemen. I'm Cindy.

I would like to introduce the packing of lemon slicers exported to France.

As for the inner packing, 1 piece is packed into an OPP bag. Bags must have 5 mm small holes for air in and out. Six Silica gel bags will be inserted into an OPP bag. And then each piece is put into a white gift box. Information including names of commodity, importer, lot, etc., will be printed on each gift box. And this food-grade logo must be over 10 mm high.

Finally, 48 pieces are packed into an outer carton. A grade corrugate cardboard carton will be used, because if broken cartons arrive in Europe, they will be rejected by customers. Besides, glue is allowed for carton and metal staples are forbidden.

Each carton must be marked with the details including:

(1) Weight. The Net Weight should be 13 kg and the Gross weight 15 kg.

(2) Symbols of warnings like "Keep Dry".

(3) Directions like "Open here".

(4) "Recycle" is printed on the front side.

In addition, we will add pallets on the floor of container to protect against water. That's all.

Thank you. Any questions?

> 根据上述的介绍，请你完成如下的学习任务：

记录同学有关包装汇报要点：

Reporter:	Name of product:
Detailed information	1. 2. 3.
I suggest	
I ask	
I learn	

备注：欢迎大家登录课程的在线平台，点击观看往届学生的任务展示及教师点评。

扫一扫

6.4.2 模拟同客户沟通产品包装的任务

在这个学习任务中，每个分配到任务的学习小组将根据课程的学习模拟就某一特定产品的包装展开沟通的任务。要求具体如下：

①设计、布置表演场景。

②准备相关资料，比如样品、内包装的礼盒、气泡袋、纸板等；有些包装信息可以通过电脑、图片等方式引入。

③在包装介绍时要注意：一定要结合具体的产品来介绍包装。销售包装、运输包装的材料、颜色、方法以及注意事项要符合目标市场及运输方式。英语用词要专业、准确。另外，恰当地使用肢体语言来更好地支持你们的沟通和交流。

④请正装出镜；请在任务中脱稿表演。

⑤在视频的后期制作中，对于产品包装中涉及的某些陌生的专业词汇请在视频中以中英文字幕的形式出现，方便大家学习。

> 根据上述的介绍，请你完成如下的学习任务：

记录有关小组包装沟通任务的要点：

The team:	Name of product:
Detailed information	1. 2. 3.
I suggest	
I think	
I learn	

备注：欢迎大家登录课程的在线平台，点击观看往届学生的任务展示及教师点评。

扫一扫

6.4.3 模拟沟通包装的即兴任务

在这个任务中，模拟与客户就包装展开进一步磋商的工作任务。由于包装不当也会影响履约，我们在对外贸易中要充分重视出口包装。任务的要点是：卖家能把产品常用的包装介绍清楚，买家基于卖家的介绍要提出自己对包装的特殊要求和建议。在本即兴表演中，随机搭配的小组分别扮演客户和卖家，扮演客户的A组在任务中重在了解卖家的产品包装，并提出相应的包装要求；扮演卖家的B组在任务中介绍常用的出口包装情况，并根据客户的市场要求进行相应的改进。

> **根据上述的介绍，请你完成如下的学习任务：**

❶ 团队根据分配到的任务编号学习相关的包装沟通的信息单。

❷ 团队分配任务，根据相关的产品包装信息搜集相关的文字和图片资料并完成准备。

❸ 在即兴任务进行时，请在同伴小组的任务单下记录相关的信息并做必要的评价。

> 即兴任务附件

No.1

Team A (the buyer)

Packing Requirements for Foldable Led Light	
Inner packing	Color Box, Blister Shell[1], Display[2], Gift Box
Outer packing	____PCS/CTN
Measurement	
Gross weight	
Additional requests for packing	Place of origin

Team B (the seller)

Packing Information of Foldable Led Light	
Inner packing	Color Box, Blister Shell[1], Display[2], Gift Box
Outer packing	50 PCS/CTN
Packing detail	
Color	
Measurement	43 cm*27.5 cm*57 cm=0.067 cbm
Gross weight	15 KGS
Package can be customized	

备注：1. Blister Shell：吸塑壳；2. Display：展示盒

No.2

Team A (the buyer)

Packing Requirements for Color Pencil	
Quantity	
Inner packing	OPP Bag, PVC Bag, Paper Box, Blister Card
Outer packing	
Specification	2.65/2.85/3.0 mm[1]
Lead color	
Additional requests for packing	Warnings
	Bar code

Team B (the seller)

Packing Information of Color Pencil	
Quantity	
Usual package	OPP Bag, PVC Bag, Paper Box, Blister Card
Packing option	30,000 PCS for bulk pack, 5,000 sets for set packing like blister, PVC case, color box
Specification	2.65/2.85/3.0 mm[1] and other sizes
Lead color	Up to 120 colors
Lead hardness	6b, 5b, 4b, 3b, 2b, B, F, H, 2h, 3h, 4h, 5h
Package can be customized	

备注：1. 铅芯直径

No.3

Team A (the buyer)

Packing Requirements for Ceramic Coffee Mug	
Quantity	8, 000 PCS
Inner packing	PP Bag +Inner Box +Carton
Outer packing	
Specification	____ oz[1]
Color	
Additional requests for packing	Layers on carton

Team B (the seller)

Packing Information of Ceramic Coffee Mug	
Inner packing	PP Bag; Inner Box; Gift Box
Color	customized
Outer packing	12 PCS/egg tray, 36 PCS/carton
Packing detail	
Specification	promotional ceramic mugs can be 11 oz,or 12 oz
Cup accessories	with handle
Package can be customized	

备注：1.oz指盎司，1 oz=28.35 g

No.4

Team A (the buyer)

Packing Requirements for Metal Belt Buckle[1]	
Inner packing	
Outer packing	
Plating option	
Specification	
Additional requests for packing	The sealing method for cartons: adhesive

Team B (the seller)

Packing Information of Metal Belt Buckle	
Inner packing	polybag, Gift Box, Velvet, Card, Plastic Box or as client request
Outer packing	1 PC/polybag, 50 PCS/small box, 300 PCS/CNT
Packing detail	
Specification	40–60 mm diameter(直径)
Plating option	gold, silver, nickel, brass, copper, antique plating, misty plating, dual plating[2]
Package can be customized	

备注：1. 金属皮带扣；2. 上述材质分别为金、银、镍、黄铜、铜、仿古电镀、电镀镀雾、双镀

No.5

Team A (the buyer)

Packing Requirements for Men Polo Shirt	
Quantity	16, 000 PCS
Inner packing	OPP Bag, Gift Box
Outer packing	
Trademark	
Size	
Color	
Additional requests for packing	Ventilation holes

Team B (the seller)

Packing Information of Men Polo Shirt	
Inner packing	OPP Bag, Gift Box or as your requirements
Outer packing	50 PCS/CTN
Packing detail	
Quantity	
Size	XS, S, M, L, XL, XXL, XXXL
Color	As per your instruction
Trademark:	Newstar Polo Shirt
Package can be customized	

No.6

Team A (the buyer)

Packing Requirements of 3-Fold Manual Umbrella	
Quantity	60, 000 PCS
Inner packing	
Outer packing	
Material	pongee
Color	green, blue, purple
Additional requests for packing	Silica gel

Team B (the seller)

Packing Information of 3-Fold Manual Umbrella	
Inner packing	OPP bag, Pouch, Gift Box
Outer packing	72 PCS/CTN
Packing detail	
Material	pongee
Color	customized
Logo	
Package can be customized	

项目7 沟通装运

学习目标

知识目标

1. 了解货物延期装运造成的后果及规避方法；
2. 理解货物装运沟通的要点和难点；
3. 掌握货物装运的英语表述和沟通策略。

能力目标

1. 能够根据货物装运主题搜集相关的资料；
2. 掌握如何同目标国客户就装运展开有效沟通；
3. 能够明确货物装运沟通要点并完成情景模拟任务。

任务 7.1 认识出口装运

货物在出口装运中，按期将合同规定的货物装上运输工具或交给承运人是履约的重要体现。同时，在国际贸易中时间成本特别昂贵，客户敲定的时间很大程度上是为了迎合当地的销售时间。为了避免延误航班、班列、船期及出现漫长的等待时间，我们要做到每个环节都在进程上。根据相关外贸业务员的反馈，不少订单的纠纷就是因为货物赶不上装运期造成。因此，我们要重视积极规避这类问题的发生。

> 根据上述的介绍，请你完成如下的学习任务：

❶ 概括延期装运的后果：

❷ 分析企业赔空运的原因：

❸ 归纳应对延期装运的方法：

1.	
2.	

列举可行的解决方案：

❹ 总结避免延期交货的方法：

1.	
2.	
3.	
4.	

任务 7.2 分析装运沟通案例

7.2.1 介绍案例产品：出口圣诞树

圣诞节已成为西方世界以及其他很多信仰基督教地区的公共假日。圣诞树象征着上帝赐予的永远的生命，已然成为圣诞节必不可少的一种节日装饰品。现在，仿真圣诞树风格各异、树形大小不一、灯色鲜艳、装饰物琳琅满目，深受国外消费者的青睐和喜爱。浙江义乌占据了全球圣诞用品80%的市场份额，形成了圣诞用品生产、销售、包装等环节的产业链。

> 根据上述的介绍，请你完成如下的学习任务：

❶ 概况圣诞树的材质及树形特点：

❷ 列举常见圣诞树的电压插头：

❸ 分析圣诞树饰品种类和特点：

❹ 分析生产企业的每年工作进程：

时间	工作进程
1. 春交会	
2.	
3.	

扫一扫

7.2.2 装运沟通案例

【案例背景介绍】

Lois在义乌的一家贸易型的外贸礼品企业工作，她在3月份接了很多的圣诞树及饰品的订单，7月、8月不断跟进客人的订单。这几天，她的一票去英国的圣诞树的订单出现了状况，工厂方面要求增加10天的生产期，这导致她无法赶上同英国客人Tedeas约定的船期。因此，她及时联系了客人，说明了情况，并同客人沟通解决的办法。

Lois: Hello, this is Lois Lee from Yiwu Golden-times Gifts & Crafts Co., Ltd.

Tedeas: Hello, Lois.

Lois: Yeah. Today, I call to inform you that we cannot deliver your Christmas trees and balls on time. And I'm very sorry for that.

Tedeas: What's wrong?

Lois: Because our manufacturer has received a lot of orders in spite of a labor shortage since July, so they cannot catch up with the shipping date. Could you give me another 10 days?

Tedeas: Lois, another 10 days means we will miss the best-selling season. I'm afraid that I cannot accept that.

Lois: Ok, I see. Then I have to contact other manufacturers to catch up the production plan. I will send you the new samples.

Tedeas: Oh, that will be good.

Lois: Ok, good. By the way, will you accept partial shipments?

Tedeas: Partial shipments?

Lois: Yes. I will send the first lot by sea, and the rest by priority express.

Tedeas: In such case, when is the earliest shipment I can expect?

Lois: The first lot of goods will arrive on the date you have asked for. And the second lot will only take another 18 days to be delivered directly to your supermarket. In the way, I believe you will not miss the selling season.

Tedeas: How about the cost?

Lois: Don't worry. The cost is cheap and will be on us. It will not bring you some trouble. Do you prefer a new manufacturer or partial shipments?

Tedeas: Let me see. So I think priority express will be better.

Lois: Yes, it has been proved to be safe and punctual.

Tedeas: I have to accept your suggestion, since there is no better solution.

Lois: Good, good. Thank you very much for your understanding. I assure you that I will handle the partial shipments as we have discussed. I will book the shipping space by sea and by priority express, and soon I will send you the revised order by email as well.

Tedeas: Ok, good.

Lois: Again, please accept my sincere apology. Thank you for your help and understanding. Goodbye.

Tedeas: Goodbye.

> 根据上述的案例，请你完成如下的学习任务：

❶ 请把加框的单词填入表格并注上中文，并把画线的句子翻译在原文处。

1.	2.	3.	4.
5.	6.	7.	8.

❷ 重点跟读加框的单词、画线的句子并能准确、流利地读出来、说出来。

7.2.3 理解装运沟通案例

扫一扫

产品进入大货生产后会出现各种问题，需要我们及时跟进并加以解决。圣诞礼品这类季节性较强的货物订单往往会出现工厂无法完成既定的生产计划、赶不上交期的情况。交期延误不仅影响了客户的销售，也会损害出口商的商誉，不利于双方今后的合作。那么，如何把延误的时间抢回来，争取按期交货呢？请大家跟随我们的课程一起进入今天的学习内容。

> 根据上述的介绍，请你完成如下的学习任务：

❶ 归纳 Lois 延期交货的理由：

❷ 总结 Lois 面对延期交货提出的方案：

方案 1	
方案 2	
方案 3	

❸ 分析优先性快递优点：

❹ 谈谈 Lois 的案例给你的启发：

7.2.4 分析英国市场及客户

英国四面环海，隔北海、多佛尔海峡、英吉利海峡与欧洲大陆相望。传统的英国人注重生活质量，在重要场合往往穿着正规，特别喜爱阳光、外出旅游度假。英国历史悠久，国民爱好各类文化活动，例如阅读书刊、写作、听音乐会、看戏剧等，英国也因绅士风度而闻名遐迩。中英两国贸易往来历史悠久，近年来随着中国“一带一路”倡议的推进以及英国“脱欧”的影响，中英贸易关系更加紧密。

> 根据上述的介绍，请你完成如下的学习任务：

❶ 列举英国的概况：

❷ 分析英国市场特点：

❸ 分析英国客户特点：

❹ 谈谈本视频给你的启发：

❺ 补充英国市场及客户分析：

任务 7.3 分析装运沟通拓展案例

扫一扫

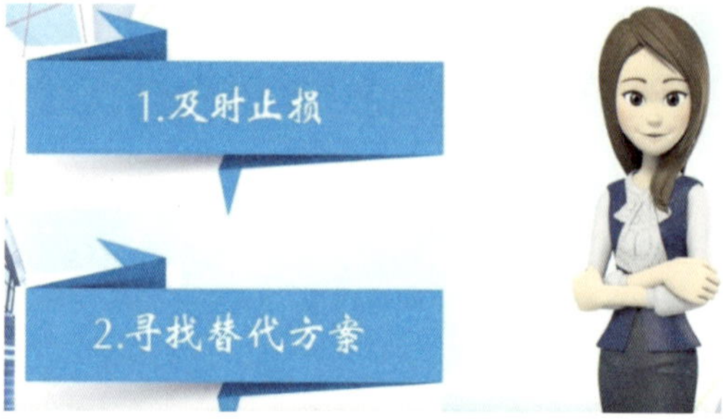

10% 的订单因为交期问题而令业务员焦头烂额：延迟交货可能导致货物的无理由拒收甚至付出惨痛的代价。今天我们分享一个有关“不能按时装运”的案例。Alice 就职于杭州一家文具出口企业，她负责跟进的这个订单是来自土耳其的大客户的一票圆珠笔订单，客人要求2017年8月15日前装运，但是2017年4月开始的浙江环保执法对当地电镀厂影响很大，导致该订单无法按进度生产。Alice 是如何应对的呢？希望这则小案例能带给大家在细节上的一些启发和思考。

> 根据上述的介绍，请你完成如下的学习任务：

❶ 归纳 Alice 分析处理订单延期实际情况：

1.	
2.	
3.	

❷ 分析 Alice 沟通新的装运时间时存在的问题：

❸ 总结 Alice 同老板沟通后的处理方案：

❹ 谈谈拓展案例给你的启发：

任务 7.4 模拟装运沟通任务

7.4.1 模拟介绍出口产品交货方案的任务

按约定的条件交货是履约的重要体现，在这次任务中我们主要是汇报某一外贸订单的交货方案。

首先，请介绍外贸订单的背景信息，包括订单的产品、数量、下单时间等。

其次，制订合理的交货方案，具体包括运输方式、装运时间、承运人、起运港和目的港等。此外，也要具体说明是否允许分批装运、转运等细节。

【参考例文】

A Delivery Plan of Goods

Hello,everyone. I'm Simon. Today I will make a report about the delivery plan of the beach bikes under Contract No.784. Our old client placed an order of 2, 000 sets in early March.

As for delivery plan, we will arrange marine transportation in this way. We will ship the goods by MSK before 15th April from Shenzhen to Miami. According to our client's requests, transshipment and partial shipment will not be allowed.

Besides, this client adds that any delay of delivery more than 10 days, the supplier will afford the transportation expenses; any delay of delivery more than 20 days, the buyer will refuse the order and ask for returning the paid deposit.

Therefore, it's very important for us to carry out the production plan on time and book the shipping space in advance. That's all.

Thank you! Any questions?

> 根据上述的介绍，请你完成如下的学习任务：

记录同学有关发货的汇报要点：

Reporter:	Name of product:
Detailed information	1. 2. 3.
I suggest	
I ask	
I learn	

备注：欢迎大家登录课程的在线平台，点击观看往届学生的任务展示及教师点评。

扫一扫

7.4.2　模拟同客户就交期变动展开沟通的任务

同学们，下面我来简要地介绍下“模拟同客户就交期变动展开沟通”的情景表演任务。在这个学习任务中，每个分配到任务的学习小组将根据课程的学习，模拟某一出口产品的交期变动沟通的任务。要求具体如下：

①设计、布置表演场景。交期发生临时变动是外贸货物出口中发生频率比较高的事件，因此设置在线沟通比较合理，并呈现出一定的商务背景。大家可以考虑如何利用学校及周边的场地进行设置。

②准备相关资料，比如产品合同等的相关文件资料。

③在客户提出改变交期的沟通中，客户方面要给出新的交期时间及具体要求；出口商核实相关的信息并给出明确的回复，同时提出合理的方案和理由。另外，恰当地使用肢体语言来更好地支持你们的沟通和交流。

④请正装出镜，请在任务中脱稿表演。

> 根据上述的介绍，请你完成如下的学习任务：

记录有关小组沟通交期任务要点：

The team:	Name of product:
Detailed information	1. 2. 3.
I suggest	
I think	
I learn	

备注：欢迎大家登录课程的在线平台，点击观看往届学生的任务展示及教师点评。

7.4.3 模拟沟通装运的即兴任务

在这个任务中，模拟与客户就装运展开进一步磋商。按期装运体现了卖家履约，我们要充分重视出口装运。任务的要点是：首先，买卖双方要把与装运相关的部分信息进行确认；其次要根据各自的情况对装运进行调整；此外，对于装运的调整双方要进行协调和沟通。在本即兴表演中，随机搭配的小组分别扮演客户和卖家，扮演客户的A组可以根据订单的市场就装运提出新的要求并和对方进行协商；扮演卖家的B组可以根据订单实际生产和订舱等情况就装运提出新的调整并和对方进行协商。

> 根据上述的介绍，请你完成如下的学习任务：

❶ 团队根据分配到的任务编号学习相关的装运沟通的信息单。

❷ 团队分配任务，根据相关的产品装运信息搜集相关的文字和图片资料并完成准备工作。

❸ 在即兴任务进行时，请在同伴小组的任务单下记录相关的信息并做必要的评价。

即兴任务附件

No.1

Team A (the buyer)

Shipment for Felt[1] Hat for Christmas Party	
Article No.	HP–HWD015
Quantity	500, 000 PCS
Packing	1 PC/OPP bag, 500 PCS/CTN
Production time	2–15 days
Transshipment	allowed prohibited
Port of destination	
Date of shipment	On or before Sept. 15
What is revised	

Team B (the seller)

Shipment for Felt[1] Hat for Christmas Party	
Article No.	HP–HWD015
Quantity	500, 000 PCS
Packing	1 PC/OPP bag, 500 PCS/CTN
Production time	2–15 days
Shipping	2–15 days after receiving 30% deposit
Port of departure	
Date of shipment	On or before Sept. 15
What is revised	

备注：1. felt：毛毡，用毛制成的纺织品

No.2

Team A (the buyer)

Shipment for Dog house	
Article No.	ACC-2013
Quantity	30, 000 PCS
Packing	1 piece for a polybag, and in an export carton
Production time	25-30 days
Transshipment	allowed prohibited
Port of destination	
Date of shipment	Before Oct. 20
What is revised	

Team B (the seller)

Shipment for Dog house	
Article No.	ACC-2013
Quantity	30, 000 PCS
Packing	1 piece for a polybag, and in an export carton
Production time	25-30 days
Shipping	25-30 days after receiving 30% deposit
Port of departure	
Date of shipment	Before Oct. 20
What is revised	

No.3

Team A (the buyer)

Shipment for Vacuum Flask	
Article No.	MT–B002H
Quantity	12, 000 PCS
Packing	1 piece/color box 36 PCS/carton
Production time	15–20 days
Transshipment	allowed prohibited
Port of destination	
Date of shipment	At the end of May
What is revised	

Team B (the seller)

Shipment for Vacuum Flask	
Article No.	MT–B002H
Quantity	12, 000 PCS
Packing	1 PC/color box 36 PCS/carton
Production time	15–20 days
Shipping	15–20 days after receiving 30% deposit
Port of departure	
Date of shipment	At the end of May
What is revised	?% more or less

No.4

Team A (the buyer)

Shipment for Sports Socks	
Article No.	JHB–11093A
Quantity	100, 000 PCS
Packing	1 pair/polybag, 6 pairs/small box, 36 pairs/CNT
Production time	10–25 days
Partial shipment	allowed prohibited
Port of destination	
Date of shipment	Before Mar. 10
What is revised	

Team B (the seller)

Shipment for Sports Socks	
Article No.	JHB–11093A
Quantity	100, 000 PCS
Packing	1 pair/polybag, 6 pairs/small box, 36 pairs/CNT
Production time	10–25 days
Shipping	10–25 days after receiving 30% deposit
Port of departure	
Date of shipment	Before Mar. 10
What is revised	

No.5

Team A (the buyer)

Shipment for Paper Straw	
Article No.	ZN–465
Quantity	350, 000 PCS
Packing	50 PCS/OPP bag, 100 bags in a carton
Production time	30–45 days
Transshipment	allowed prohibited
Port of destination	
Date of shipment	During first half of Dec.
What is revised	

Team B (the seller)

Shipment for Paper Straw	
Article No.	ZN–465
Quantity	350, 000 PCS
Packing	50 PCS/OPP bag, 100 bags in a carton
Production time	30–45 days
Shipping	30–45 days after receiving 20% deposit
Port of departure	
Date of shipment	During first half of Dec.
What is revised	? % more or less

No.6

Team A (the buyer)

Shipment for Rubber Basketball	
Article No.	3FU012
Quantity	30,000 PCS
Packing	each deflated packed into an OPP bag, 60 PCS/carton
Production time	20–25days
Transshipment	allowed prohibited
Port of destination	
Date of shipment	On or about Oct. 25
What is revised	

Team B (the seller)

Shipment for Rubber Basketball	
Article No.	3FU012
Quantity	30,000 PCS
Packing	each deflated packed into an OPP bag, 60 PCS/carton
Production time	20–25 days
Shipping	20–25 days after receiving 30% deposit
Port of departure	
Date of shipment	On or about Oct. 25
What is revised	

项目8 沟通保险

学习目标

知识目标

1. 了解货物出口运输保险的种类和作用；
2. 理解货物出口运输保险沟通的要点和难点；
3. 掌握货物保险条款的英语表述和沟通策略。

能力目标

1. 能够根据货物国际运输保险的主题搜集相关的资料；
2. 能够掌握如何同目标国客户就运输保险展开有效沟通；
3. 明确货物运输保险沟通要点并完成情景模拟任务。

任务 8.1 认识出口运输保险

相较于国内贸易，国际贸易一般空间距离较远、货物运输周期较长，中途会发生各种不可控的风险。国际货物运输保险是以对外贸易货物运输过程中的各种货物作为保险标的、抵消上述风险的保险。出口货物的运输包括海运、陆运、空运以及通过邮政送递等多种途径并形成相应的四类保险，其中海运保险是四类保险中最重要的一种。一般而言，我们会同客户针对货物、航线、出口国情况就险种、期限、投保金额展开沟通。

> 根据上述的介绍，请你完成如下的学习任务：

❶ 总结出口运输保险的作用：

❷ 比较国际海运保险的种类：

种类	要点
1.	
2.	
3.	

❸ 分析合理选择险种的方法：

1.	
2.	
3.	
4.	

任务 8.2 分析保险沟通案例

扫一扫

8.2.1 介绍案例产品：出口数码印花机

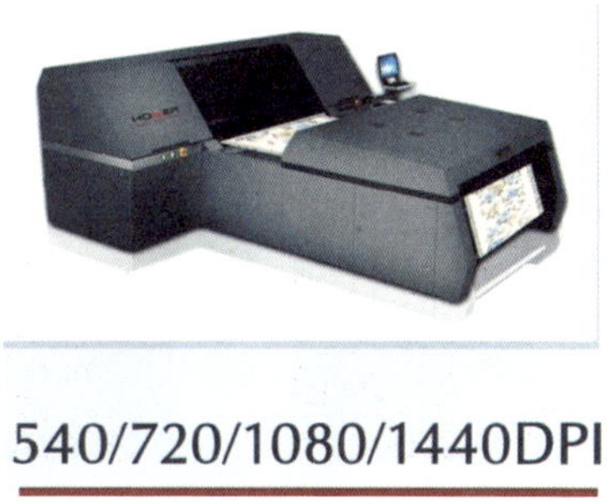

数码印花机通过墨水喷射方式进行打印和染色，不需要出菲林制版。全彩一次成像，而且定位精确、表面高保彩色图像，打印后废品率为零，很大程度上降低了生产成本，提高了织物的印刷效益。同时，这款产品也迎合了当下小批量、多品种的现代印花趋势，从而快速进入印度尼西亚、菲律宾、墨西哥、越南、印度等多个国家。

> 根据上述的介绍，请你完成如下的学习任务：

❶ 解释打印精度：

❷ 分析精度和速度的关系：

❸ 解释 PASS 值：

❹ 分析出口客户个案：

案例	特点
1. 某俄罗斯客户	
2. 某墨西哥客户	
3. 某哈萨克斯坦客户	

❺ 总结企业给国外客户的支持：

扫一扫

8.2.2 保险沟通案例

【案例背景介绍】

来自越南的客户Minh通过与Jacky的磋商最终买下了数码印花机，双方在敲定了大部分细节后，客户Minh主动提出了投保的要求。在保险事宜的沟通中，Jacky以客户为中心，在充分了解客户的投保需求的前提下确定了相关的投保事项。

Minh: Jacky, now I would like to discuss with you about the insurance for Digital Textile Printer, because I think there are many potential risks.

Jacky: Yes, I agree with you. We will arrange this for you. As our usual practice, we plan to have the goods insured with PICC.

Minh: Great. Tell me more about PICC.

Jacky: Well. It's the No.1 property insurance company in our China.

Minh: Great. I think All Risks should be appropriate for the goods.

Jacky: Well, I agree with you. No problem.

Minh: Yes, but I think, er...

Jacky: And what else should be covered?

Minh: War Risks, please.

Jacky: Ok, so the goods are to be insured against All Risks and War Risks.

Minh: And what is the insurance amount?

Jacky: It's 110% of the CIF value. What do you think?

Minh: Well, what about 130% of the CIF value.

Jacky: I'm afraid I cannot accept. Our price is already lower than that of last year due to heated competition. If you insist on 130%, I suggest the additional cost to be borne by you.

Minh: Well, how about 120%?

Jacky: Minh, 110% is commonly adopted in international trade. However we will accept the 120% insurance amount if you insist, because you are our old friend.

Minh: Well, thank you very much.

Jacky: By the way, how about the insurance period? How many days upon the discharge of the goods from the vessel?

Minh: Well, I think 60 days should be enough for the goods.

Jacky: OK, 60 days upon discharge of the insured goods from the vessel.

Minh: Thanks, Jacky.

Jacky: Minh, what else do we need to discuss about the insurance?

Minh: I think that's all.

Jacky: I will contact with PICC and arrange the insurance as we have discussed. The insurance policy will be faxed to you for confirmation.

Minh: Good, let's keep in touch.

> 根据上述的案例，请你完成如下的学习任务：

❶ 请把加框的单词填入表格并注上中文，并把画线的句子翻译在原文处。

1.	2.	3.	4.
5.	6.	7.	8.

❷ 重点跟读加框的单词、画线的句子并能准确、流利地读出来、说出来。

扫一扫

8.2.3 理解保险沟通案例

外贸的货物由于运输距离远、运输周期长，因此风险相对于内贸会更大。保险在国际贸易中发挥着降低风险的作用。在实际的操作中，对于出口货物价值比较高的产品，客人在投保时会提出较多的要求。我们在实际调研中也有不少业务员反映说，保险在出口订单的沟通中接触不多，或者几乎没有碰到过。那么，如果我们在工作中碰到了对保险有具体要求的客人，又该如何去沟通和交流呢？请大家跟随我们的课程一起进入今天的学习内容。

> 根据上述的介绍，请你完成如下的学习任务：

❶ 分析 Minh 所提议险种的合理性：

❷ 总结双方沟通后的保险要点（英文即可）：

险种	
投保金额	
期限	

❸ 归纳货物在正式投保前的注意点：

❹ 谈谈 Jacky 的做法给你的启发：

扫一扫

8.2.4 分析越南市场及客户

越南是亚洲最古老的国家之一，善于吸收外来文化，文化包容性强。一方面，越南长期深受中国文化的影响；另一方面，在法国殖民时期越南的语言、饮食、建筑等打上了法国文化的烙印。因此，越南既有东方谦虚含蓄的一面，又兼有西方奔放张扬的特点。2013 年以来，越南对外贸易一直保持高速增长，对拉动越南经济发展起到了重要作用。中越两国间交通便利，两国贸易既有竞争性又有互补性。

> 根据上述的介绍，请你完成如下的学习任务：

❶ 列举越南的概况：

❷ 分析越南市场特点：

❸ 分析越南客户特点：

❹ 谈谈本视频对你的启发：

❺ 补充越南市场及客户分析：

任务 8.3 分析保险沟通拓展案例

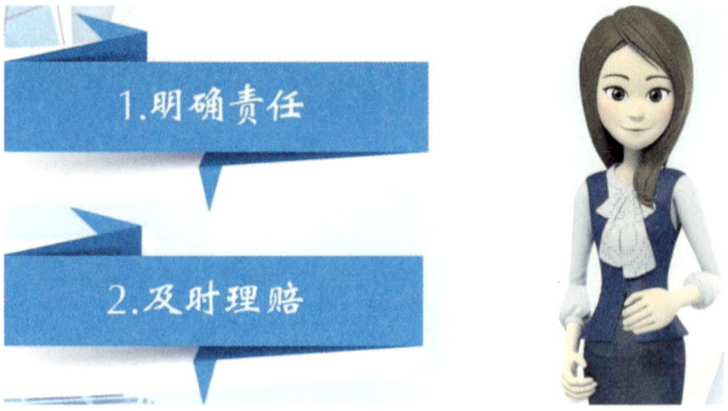

货物在国际运输中会遭遇各种风险，保险可以帮助我们转嫁运输的风险。Jack 就职于海宁一家皮革生产企业，主要负责公司在欧洲的出口业务。他经手的一票出口到荷兰的真皮手套的订单价格条件为 CIF 鹿特丹，他根据货物价值向中国人民保险公司投了一切险（ALL RISKS）。但是，买了保险就可以高枕无忧了吗？今天我们分享这则企业案例，希望这则小案例能带给大家一些启发和思考。

> 根据上述的介绍，请你完成如下的学习任务：

❶ 归纳货物到达目的港后验货的结果：

❷ 总结 Jack 在货物遭保险公司拒赔后的应对措施：

1.	
2.	
3.	

❸ 分析货物出现问题的原因：

❹ 谈谈拓展案例给你的启发：

任务8.4 模拟保险沟通任务

扫一扫

8.4.1 模拟介绍出口产品投保方案的任务

保险大大降低了国际贸易的风险。本次任务主要是汇报某一订单的投保方案。

首先，介绍订单的背景信息，尤其是涉及投保的信息，比如货物的价值，运输的方式、时间、港口、路线，以及出口的国家，等等。

其次，介绍货物具体的投保方案，包括险种、投保期限、保费、投保的公司等。

最后，根据任务的特点，选择合适的汇报呈现方式。

【参考例文】

A Plan for Transportation Insurance

Good morning. I'm Laura.

I will introduce my plan for transportation insurance. My client has ordered 1, 000 pieces of silk blouses, valued at USD 20, 000.00 to be shipped from Shanghai to Zurich, Switzerland, transshipped at Hamburg, by Maersk on CIF basis.

According to my client's instructions and our usual practice, we will get the goods insured in this way. First, we will cover insurance against All Risks and Strike Risk. Second, the insurance period is limited to fifty days upon discharge of the insured goods from the vessel. Third, the insurance will be made for 110% of the invoice value.

In addition, we will insure the goods with PICC which is always prompt in settling claims as a first-rate one. That's all.

Thank you! Any questions?

> 根据上述的介绍，请你完成如下的学习任务：

记录同学有关保险的汇报要点：

Reporter:	Name of product:
Detailed information	1. 2. 3.
I suggest	
I ask	
I learn	

备注：欢迎大家登录课程的在线平台，点击观看往届学生的任务展示及教师点评。

扫一扫

8.4.2　模拟同客户就投保展开沟通的任务

同学们，下面我来简要地介绍下“模拟就客户提出的投保要求展开沟通”的情景表演任务。在这个学习任务中，每个分配到本任务的学习小组将根据课程的学习模拟商讨某一订单的投保任务。要求具体如下：

①设计、布置保险条款的沟通表演场景。大家可以考虑如何利用学校及周边的场地进行设置。

②准备相关资料，比如产品合同、保单等的相关文件资料。

③在沟通中：首先，客户方面要给出投保的具体要求；出口商则要结合订单以及货物的特点，就险种、期限、保费等条款和客户进行商议。最后，双方在投保方案上达成一致意见。此外，出口商要注意保单填写后要请客户确认。

④请在任务中脱稿表演。

> 根据上述的介绍，请你完成如下的学习任务：

记录有关小组沟通保险任务的要点：

The team:	Name of product:
Detailed information	1. 2. 3.
I suggest	
I think	
I learn	

备注：欢迎大家登录课程的在线平台，点击观看往届学生的任务展示及教师点评。

扫一扫

8.4.3 模拟沟通保险的即兴任务

在这个任务中，模拟你方与客户就保险展开进一步磋商的工作任务。保险一方面可以转移货物在国际贸易中的风险，另一方面也会增加出口的成本。任务的要点是买卖双方要把货物与保险相关的部分信息进行确认，其次要根据货物、航线、港口、目标市场等实际情况对保险条款进行调整。在本即兴表演中，随机搭配的小组分别扮演客户和卖家，扮演客户的A组根据实际情况就保险提出要求，并和对方进行协商；扮演卖家的B组要根据订单价格、成本等实际情况就保险条款和对方进行积极协商。

> 根据上述的介绍，请你完成如下的学习任务：

❶ 团队根据分配到的任务编号学习相关的保险沟通的信息单。

❷ 团队分配任务，根据相关的产品保险信息搜集相关的文字和图片资料并完成准备工作。

❸ 在即兴任务进行时，请在同伴小组的任务单下记录相关的信息并做必要的评价。

> 即兴任务附件

No.1

Team A (the buyer)

Transportation Insurance for Crystal Ashtray	
Contract No.	CGCA2017-1201
Unit price	USD____/PC CIF
Insurance company	PICC
Claim payable at	
Risks covered	
Insurance amount	
Period	60 days after the discharge of goods
Unloading port	

Team B (the seller)

Transportation Insurance for Crystal Ashtray	
Contract No.	CGCA2017-1201
Unit price	USD____/PC CIF
Insurance company	PICC
Claim payable at	
Risks covered	
Insurance amount	110% of CIF value
Ports	Loading port: Ningbo
	Unloading port:
Period	60 days after the discharge of goods

No.2

Team A (the buyer)

Transportation Insurance for Wallpaper	
Contract No.	SAC2014-107
Insurance company	PICC
Claim payable at	
Risks covered	
Insurance amount	
Period	60 days after the discharge of goods
Unloading port	

Team B (the seller)

Transportation Insurance for Wallpaper	
Contract No.	SAC2014-107
Insurance company	PICC
Claim payable at	
Risks covered	
Insurance amount	
Ports	Loading port: Shanghai
	Unloading port:
Period	60 days after the discharge of goods

No.3

Team A (the buyer)

Transportation Insurance for Smart Mobile Phone	
Contract No.	BH2008-654
Insurance company	PICC
Claim payable at	
Risks covered	
Insurance amount	
Period	60 days after the discharge of goods
Unloading port	

Team B (the seller)

Transportation Insurance for Smart Mobile Phone	
Contract No.	BH2008-654
Insurance company	PICC
Claim payable at	
Risks covered	
Insurance amount	
Ports	Loading port: Tianjin
	Unloading port:
Period	60 days after the discharge of goods

No.4

Team A (the buyer)

Transportation Insurance for LED Flashlight	
Contract No.	NK2011–23
Unit price	USD8.5/PC CIF Tartus
Insurance company	PICC
Claim payable at	
Risks covered	
Insurance amount	
Period	60 days after the discharge of goods
Unloading port	Tartus

Team B (the seller)

Transportation Insurance for LED Flashlight	
Contract No.	NK2011–23
Unit price	USD8.5/PC CIF Tartus
Insurance company	PICC
Claim payable at	
Risks covered	
Insurance amount	
Ports	Loading port:
	Unloading port: Tartus
Period	60 days after the discharge of goods

No.5

Team A (the buyer)

Transportation Insurance for Shoes	
Contract No.	XU2006-15
Price	USD8/pair CIF Fos
Insurance company	PICC
Claim payable at	
Risks covered	
Insurance amount	
Period	60 days after the discharge of goods
Unloading port	Fos

Team B (the seller)

Transportation Insurance for Shoes	
Contract No.	XU2006-15
Price	USD8/pair CIF Fos
Insurance company	PICC
Claim payable at	
Risks covered	
Insurance amount	
Ports	Loading port:
	Unloading port: Fos
Period	60 days after the discharge of goods

No.6

Team A (the buyer)

Transportation Insurance for Peanuts	
Contract No.	JX2014-634
Insurance company	PICC
Claim payable at	
Risks covered	
Insurance amount	
Period	60 days after the discharge of goods
Unloading port	New York

Team B (the seller)

Transportation Insurance for Peanuts	
Contract No.	JX2014-634
Insurance company	PICC
Claim payable at	
Risks covered	
Insurance amount	
Ports	Loading port:
	Unloading port: New York
Period	60 days after the discharge of goods

项目9 沟通支付

学习目标

知识目标

1. 了解国际支付的作用和特点；
2. 理解国际支付沟通的要点和难点；
3. 掌握国际支付英语表述和沟通策略。

能力目标

1. 能够根据国际支付的主题搜集相关的资料；
2. 掌握如何同目标国客户就国际支付展开有效沟通；
3. 明确模拟国际支付沟通的要点并完成模拟任务。

任务9.1 认识国际支付

随着世界商品生产和流通的高度发展，产生了多种国际支付方式。如今，国际贷款的收付已由现货交易逐渐演变为以买卖双方通过银行或其他中介进行结算为特征的各种支付方式。随着各国商品交换力度的加强和范围的扩大，收汇风险成了国际商贸最主要的风险之一。因此，为了抵消收汇风险、平衡客户利益，各个企业会结合自身的实际情况和经验灵活采用不同的支付方式。

> 根据上述的介绍，请你完成如下的学习任务：

❶ 列举常见的支付方式：

❷ 总结影响国际支付选择的要点：

❸ 比较重要的国际支付方式：

支付方式	优势
1. 信用证	
2. 前 T/T	
3. 赊销	

任务9.2 分析支付沟通案例

9.2.1 介绍案例产品：出口竹地板

我国是世界上竹材资源较为丰富的国家，长江以南生长着世界上85%的毛竹。竹材属于速生材，符合当下国际的环保潮流。竹地板作为一种新型建筑装饰材料，经过二十几道工序加工而成，产品在实际应用中有着不同于实木地板和强化地板的鲜明特色和优势。竹地板作为一款有中国特色的地板种类深受海外消费者的青睐，据统计我国的竹地板约60%—70%出口到国外市场，尤其在欧美和部分东南亚市场受到广泛的欢迎。

> 根据上述的介绍，请你完成如下的学习任务：

❶ 概括主要的工序：

❷ 分析竹地板的优势：

❸ 比较竹地板种类：

种类	加工方法
1.	
2.	
3.	

❹ 总结主要出口指标：

9.2.2 支付沟通案例

【案例背景介绍】

Rose公司是美国一家规模很大的家具经销商，也是Bruce公司合作多年的大客户。Rose公司方面为了更好地实现对全球供应商的管理，在订单预定和支付方面实施全新的管理和改变。经过前期的邮件、电话沟通后，双方最后在中方的公司谈妥了新的支付条件。

Bruce: Hi, Rose, nice to meet you again. Take a seat, please.

Rose: Thanks. Today I come here to negotiate the payment of bamboo flooring for our future cooperation.

Bruce: Yeah, I see. We have studied your new payment conditions since I got your email two weeks ago.

Rose: Fine, thanks. Then would you please tell me your ideas?

Bruce: As you know, for the two years of cooperation, you have been using T/T for payment, 30% as deposit, and 70% after shipment. Your payment records are very good.

Rose: Yes, of course. We are a big and mature company in America. Bruce, will you accept O/A payment and join the Booking System?

Bruce: O/A is risky but we will accept your new method of payment, because you are qualified according to the Chinese policy.

Rose: Great. Thank you very much for your trust.

Bruce: It's your good records that win our trust. How about O/A 90 days?

Rose: Well, O/A 90 days is most commonly used by our suppliers. No problem. Now can we talk about the Booking System?

Bruce: Yes, please.

Rose: This is an open and convenient system. All of our suppliers will be invited to join this system if they want to continue cooperation with us. Of course, the first step for you is to accept O/A. Then, we will send you the software installation package. All our orders will be placed through this system in the future.

Bruce: Can you show me the system?

Rose: Yes, of course. You see, after we enter this system, we will place the new order here, and you will see the information of this order in this section. You can click to accept the order or leave your comments on the price, time of delivery and anything you like. We can adjust the terms of the order accordingly. In this way, the order is placed.

Bruce: So the payment is based on the records of orders in this system?

Rose: Yes, that's right. You can set a time interval, such as 90 days and then both of us will have a list of the orders during that period. If you hand in the packing lists, the shipping documents, etc. on time, we will pay the money on time.

Bruce: Great, I'm quite clear about the system. We will join your Booking System and keep our cooperation.

Rose: Welcome. Our company plan to invite the suppliers who join our Booking System to attend the annual conference and to visit our headquarters in America.

Bruce: Good news! Thank you.

Rose: Let's meet in America next time.

> 根据上述的案例，请你完成如下的学习任务：

❶ 请把加框的单词填入表格并注上中文，并把画线的句子翻译在原文处。

1.	2.	3.	4.
5.	6.	7.	8.

❷ 重点跟读加框的单词、画线的句子并能准确、流利地读出来、说出来。

扫一扫

9.2.3 理解支付沟通案例

支付方式是国际贸易中进出口双方议定的货款结算方式。在对外贸易中，很多企业根据海外客户的信用以及企业规避风险的需求选择合适的支付方式。有些出口企业则根据实际的操作经验总结出适合企业实际情况的支付方式。同时，有些客户在长期合作中会提出调整支付方式。那么，我们在工作中如何应对客人提出的新支付方式？我们沟通和交流的重点是什么呢？请大家跟随我们的课程一起进入今天的学习。

> 根据上述的介绍，请你完成如下的学习任务：

❶ 分析 Bruce 公司接受客户赊销的原因：

❷ 总结美方推出订货系统的背景：

❸ 列举订货系统的主要功能（英文即可）：

1.	
2.	
3.	
4.	

❹ 谈谈 Bruce 公司的做法给你的启发：

扫一扫

9.2.4 分析美国市场及客户

美国在全球的政治、经济、军事、娱乐等领域有着庞大的影响力。此外，美国享有“民族大熔炉”之美誉，来自全球的移民既保留自己的文化传统又按典型的美国传统生活，使美国的人文景观呈现丰富多彩的特点。中美两国多年来经济高度融合，贸易的互补性强，贸易往来较多。

> 根据上述的介绍，请你完成如下的学习任务：

❶ 列举美国的概况：

❷ 分析美国市场特点：

❸ 分析美国客户特点：

❹ 谈谈本视频给你的启发：

❺ 补充美国市场及客户分析：

任务9.3 分析支付沟通拓展案例

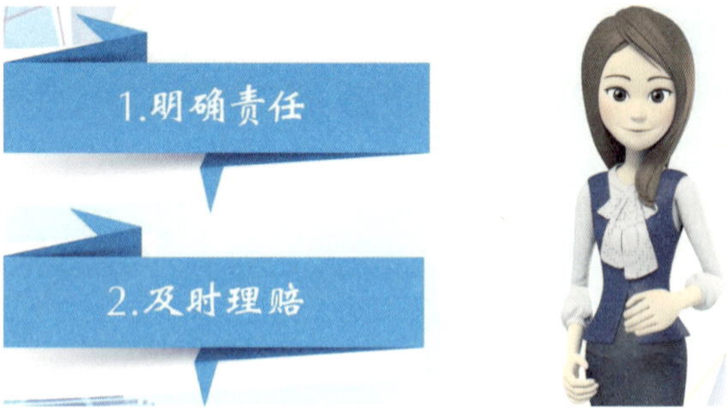

收汇风险可以说是对外贸易面临的最主要的风险。在订单的谈判中，选择合适的支付方式可以有效地规避收汇风险。Peter就职于杭州一家国营纺织出口公司，他这次经手的是美国MARY KAY公司大客户订单，即床上用品价值100万美元的毛巾订单。Peter的客人在谈合同的时候明确规定了苛刻的支付条件，他该如何应对呢？希望这则小案例能带给大家一些启发和思考。

> 根据上述的介绍，请你完成如下的学习任务：

❶ 概括大客户的特点：

❷ 列举一般的支付惯例：

1.	
2.	
3.	

❸ 分析Peter应对苛刻支付条件的方法：

❹ 谈谈拓展案例给予你的启发：

任务9.4 模拟支付沟通任务

9.4.1 模拟介绍出口产品支付方案的任务

保险大大降低了国际贸易的风险。选择合适的支付方式有助于规避风险、开拓市场。在这次任务中我们就新客户的订单提出合理的支付方案。

首先，请介绍订单的背景信息，包括产品、数量、价值、出口市场以及双方合作的前景等。

其次，请你结合上述信息提出支付方案，其中包括定金的比例、支付方式与时间等。

最后，说明采用该支付方案的理由。

【参考例文】

A Payment Plan for My New Client

Good morning, ladies and gentlemen. I'm Aby. Today, I'll share with you about my payment plan.

My new client from Britain planned to place 3,000 pieces of mountain bikes, valued at USD 450,000.00 with us. He likes our products very much and he promised to order more next time.

I suggest him that he should pay 30% of contract value for deposit by confirmed and irrevocable L/C at sight one month before shipment, and the balance by irrevocable L/C, payable at sight against presentation of shipping documents.

This is our first business with this client and the total value is quite high. As we know that L/C gives us additional protection of bank's guarantee, and this payment is also widely accepted by British clients. That's all.

Thank you! Any questions?

> 根据上述的介绍，请你完成如下的学习任务：

记录同学有关支付的汇报要点：

Reporter:	Name of product:
Detailed information	1. 2. 3.
I suggest	
I ask	
I learn	

备注：欢迎大家登录课程的在线平台，点击观看往届学生的任务展示及教师点评。

扫一扫

9.4.2　模拟同老客户就支付变动展开沟通的任务

在这个学习任务中，每个分配到任务的学习小组将根据课程的学习模拟商讨某一订单的投保任务。要求具体如下：

①设计、布置沟通的保险条款时表演场景。大家可以考虑如何利用学校及周边的场地进行设置。

②准备相关资料，比如产品合同、保单等相关文件资料。

③在沟通中：首先，客户方面要给出投保的具体要求；出口商则要结合订单以及货物的特点，就险种、期限、保费等条款和客户进行商议。最后，双方在投保方案上达成一致意见。此外，出口商要注意填写完保单后要请客户确认。

④请在任务中脱稿表演。

> 根据上述的介绍，请你完成如下的学习任务：

记录有关小组沟通支付任务的要点：

The team:	Name of product:
Detailed information	1. 2. 3.
I suggest	
I think	
I learn	

备注：欢迎大家登录课程的在线平台，点击观看往届学生的任务展示及教师点评。

9.4.3 模拟沟通支付的即兴任务

在这个任务中，模拟你方与客户就支付展开进一步磋商的工作任务。任务的要点是：首先，买卖双方要把与支付相关的部分信息进行确认。其次，要根据订单的情况对支付方式进行调整。此外，对于支付方式的调整要基于双方的协调和沟通。在本即兴表演中，随机搭配的小组分别扮演客户和卖家，扮演客户的A组要根据自身的利益提出优惠的支付方式，并和对方进行协商；扮演卖家的B组要根据订单等实际情况就客人的要求和对方进行协商、合理调整。

> 根据上述的介绍，请你完成如下的学习任务：

❶ 团队根据分配到的任务编号学习相关的支付沟通的信息单。

❷ 团队分配任务，根据相关的产品支付信息搜集相关的文字和图片资料并完成准备工作。

❸ 在即兴任务进行时，请在同伴小组的任务单下记录相关的信息并做必要的评价。

即兴任务附件

No.1

Team A (the buyer)

Payment for Hotel Bath Towel	
Style No.	YKY5195
Material	100% organic cotton
Specification	140cm*70cm
Quantity	
Order type	First Order
Payment	
New adjustments	

Team B (the seller)

Payment for Hotel Bath Towel	
Style No.	YKY5195
Material	100% organic cotton
Minimum order	①Usual Order: 500 pairs per style and color for stock styles ②Usual Order: 5, 000 pairs per style and color for custom style
Packing	1 pair/polybag, 200 pairs/carton
Payment	①Sample Order: 100% by T/T in advance ②First Order: 50% deposit by T/T in advance and the balance by T/T before shipment ③Repeat Order: 30% deposit by T/T in advance and the balance before shipment

No.2

Team A (the buyer)

Payment for Hourglass	
Model No.	KS29053
Material	artificial crystal
Quantity	
Order type	Repeat Order
Payment	
New adjustments	

Team B (the seller)

Payment for Hourglass	
Model No.	KS29053
Material	artificial crystal
Minimum order	100 PCS
Packing	1 piece/polybag, 300 PCS/carton
Payment	①Sample Order: 100% T/T in advance ②First Order: 40% by T/T in advance and the balance by L/C before shipment ③Repeat Order: 30% deposit by T/T, the balance before the shipment

No.3

Team A (the buyer)

Payment for Baby Car Seat	
Model No.	BBSS/8007
Material	aluminum alloy
Quantity	
Order type	Repeat Order
Payment	
New adjustments	

Team B (the seller)

Payment for Baby Car Seat	
Model No.	BBSS/8007
Material	aluminum alloy
Minimum order	1, 000 PCS
Packing	standard cartons
Payment	T/T or L/C

No.4

Team A (the buyer)

Payment for Electric Juice Extractor	
Model No.	NK2011–23
Material	stainless steel
Quantity	
Order type	Repeat Order
Payment	
New adjustments	

Team B (the seller)

Payment for Electric Juice Extractor	
Model No.	NK2011–23
Material	stainless steel
Minimum order	5 PCS per model for stock styles
Packing	1 piece/polybag, 200 PCS/carton
Payment	20% as deposit in advance by T/T, and the balance by T/T before shipment

No.5

Team A (the buyer)

Payment for Egg Cooker	
Model No.	GW-KSD01W
Material	stainless steel
Quantity	
Order type	First Order
Payment	
New Adjustment	

Team B (the seller)

Payment for Egg Cooker	
Model No.	GW-KSD01W
Material	stainless steel
Minimum order	500 PCS per each model and color for stock models
Packing	One in color box and one dozen in a carton
Payment	L/C, T/T, Western Union

No.6

Team A (the buyer)

Payment for Rubber Flip Flops	
Style No.	L–4020
Material	Outsole: EVA; Upper: PVC
Quantity	
Order type	Repeat Order
Payment	
New adjustments	

Team B (the seller)

Payment for Rubber Flip Flops	
Style No.	L–4020
Material	Outsole: EVA; Upper: PVC
Minimum order	300 PCS
Packing	1 pair/polybag/box, 50 pairs/carton or as customers' requirements
Payment	L/C, T/T(30% deposit and 70% against the copy of B/L), Paypal, Western Union, MoneyGram, Esrow

项目10 沟通合同签订

学习目标

知识目标

1. 了解出口合同内容、注意事项；

2. 理解出口合同沟通的要点和难点；

3. 掌握出口合同英语表述和沟通策略。

能力目标

1. 能够根据出口合同签订的主题搜集相关的资料；

2. 掌握如何同目标国客户就合同签订展开有效沟通；

3. 明确模拟出口合同签订要点并完成情景模拟任务。

任务10.1 认识出口合同

出口合同是进口商、出口商依法通过协商就双方在贸易的权利和义务上所达成的具有法律约束力的书面协议，也称为销售确认书（sales confirmation）或销售合同（sales contract）。依法签订后，它是双方履约的依据，也是对贸易纠纷进行调节、仲裁、诉讼等的法律依据。因此，我们要充分重视出口合同的起草、修订、签订等环节，力争赢在双方合作的起跑线上。

> 根据上述的介绍，请你完成如下的学习任务：

❶ 概括出口合同的作用：

❷ 比较案例合同特点：

合同	特点
合同1（俄罗斯客户）	
合同2（　　　　）	
合同3（　　　　）	
合同4（　　　　）	

❸ 总结起草合同应具备的能力：

❹ 列举签订合同的注意点：

任务 10.2 分析沟通签订合同案例

扫一扫

10.2.1 介绍案例产品：出口围巾

围巾有长条形、三角形、方形等，一般采用羊毛、棉、丝等天然材质，或是莫代尔、人棉、腈纶、涤纶等化纤以及混纺。消费者一般为了保暖、美观、团队活动等而穿戴，产品属于服装的配件，出口企业往往根据目标国消费群体的不同需求采用不同的材质、上色方法和设计。多年来，中国的企业逐渐形成了产业基地，在生产规模、价格、设计上形成了较为强劲的出口优势。

> 根据上述的介绍，请你完成如下的学习任务：

❶ 归纳围巾的上色方法：

❷ 分析品牌客户的要求：

1. 面料	
2. 上色	
3. 标准	

❸ 评价品牌客户控制成本的方法：

扫一扫

10.2.2 合同签订沟通案例

【案例背景介绍】

杨先生在杭州一家工贸一体的真丝产品的企业从事出口业务。最近，他和加拿大客户 Jackie 的订单谈判进展顺利。Jackie 在到中国走访各供应商期间和杨先生约好时间来公司签署合同。他们在签约前就合同中存在争议的条款展开磋商、认真审核了合同条款并最后签下了合同。

Mr. Yang: Good morning, Jackie. I'm glad that we are about to sign the sales contract of silk scarves with item No. MK-549A, MK-549B and MK-549C after our discussion.

Jackie: Me too. I'm happy with the progress we have made these days. Can we sign the contract today?

Mr. Yang: Yes, let's get down to business. You sent me the email the other day to add another 6, 000 PCS in the current order, 2, 000 for each item. I have checked with our factory and they told me that they cannot finish before the shipping date. You know they are too busy with orders these days.

Jackie: I'm sorry to hear that but I really want a bigger order.

Mr. Yang: Well, can you accept partial shipments? If so, we can deliver you the first lot as we discussed before, and the additional 6, 000 PCS by air within 40 days afterwards. In this way, you will not miss the selling seasons.

Jackie: How about the cost of air transportation?

Mr. Yang: Well, we can share it equally.

Jackie: Thanks and I accept partial shipments.

Mr. Yang: Next, let's talk about the price for 6,000 PCS. As the costs of labor and raw materials have been rising quickly, we want to keep the right to adjust the price by an amount equal to the increase in cost. I hope you can understand our situation.

Jackie: I see. But I'm not sure whether we can still accept the price after your adjustment. We can put it this way: The Seller reserves the right to adjust the price by an amount equal to the increase in cost incurred after the date of this order due to factors outside the control of the Seller, subject to written consent from the Buyer. If the Buyer does not accept the price adjustment, the contract shall be cancelled. What do you think?

Mr. Yang: Er, your suggestion is reasonable. We would like to accept your proposal.

Jackie: Good.

Mr. Yang: By the way I think it's better to add a more or less clause here, so that our factory can control the production.

Jackie: How many percentages do you ask for?

Mr. Yang: 5% less both in quantity and amount per item will be acceptable.

Jackie: 3%.

Mr. Yang: Fine, I agree. Do you have anything to add or adjust?

Jackie: No, thanks.

...

Mr. Yang: Jackie, let's enjoy some fruits.

Secretary: I have revised the contract based on your discussion.

Mr. Yang: Thank you.

Jackie: Thank you.

Mr. Yang: Thanks. Jackie, finally we have agreed on the terms of the contract. Before we sign, let's check the relevant terms and clauses again.

Jackie: Ok. Let me see, unit price12 dollars per piece CIF Vancouver, quantity 18,000 PCS, partial shipments... Correct!

Mr. Yang: So we've settled the terms for the contract. Let's sign the contract.

Jackie: Yes, please!

Mr. Yang: Thank you.

> 根据上述的案例，请你完成如下的学习任务：

❶ 请把加框的单词填入表格并注上中文，并把画线的句子翻译在原文处。

1.	2.	3.	4.
5.	6.	7.	8.

❷ 重点跟读加框的单词、画线的句子并能准确、流利地读出来、说出来。

扫一扫

10.2.3　理解合同签订沟通案例

外贸合同对买卖双方的责任、权利、义务、费用和风险等进行了明确的划分。在对外贸易中，虽然双方经过深入沟通并达成订单、合同，他们也会因为种种变化对合同进行调整。那么，如果我们在工作中遇到新的情况，如何在争取客户的同时兼顾企业的利益？如何做出积极、合理的应对？我们沟通和交流的重点是什么呢？请大家跟随我们的课程一起进入今天的学习内容。

> 根据上述的介绍，请你完成如下的学习任务：

❶ 归纳杨先生应对客户追加订单的方法：

❷ 解释“开放式合同”：

❸ 列举“溢短装”条款的作用：

❹ 谈谈本案例给你的启发：

扫一扫

10.2.4 分析加拿大市场及客户

加拿大地域辽阔、美丽富饶，国土面积达998万平方千米，位居世界第二。加拿大丰富的自然资源、高度发达的科技使其成为生活水准高、社会富裕、经济发达的国家。作为典型的移民国家，加拿大聚集了来自世界各地不同的人群，文化上也呈现出多元的特点。同时，加拿大以贸易立国，外贸依存度高，经济上受美国的影响比较深。近年来，加拿大经济增长较为强劲，增长速度在发达工业国中名列前茅。中加两国资源禀赋差异大，两国间的贸易规模和领域不断扩大。

> 根据上述的介绍，请你完成如下的学习任务：

❶ 列举加拿大的概况：

❷ 分析加拿大市场特点：

❸ 分析加拿大客户特点：

❹ 谈谈本视频给你的启发：

❺ 补充加拿大市场及客户分析：

任务10.3 分析合同沟通拓展案例

扫一扫

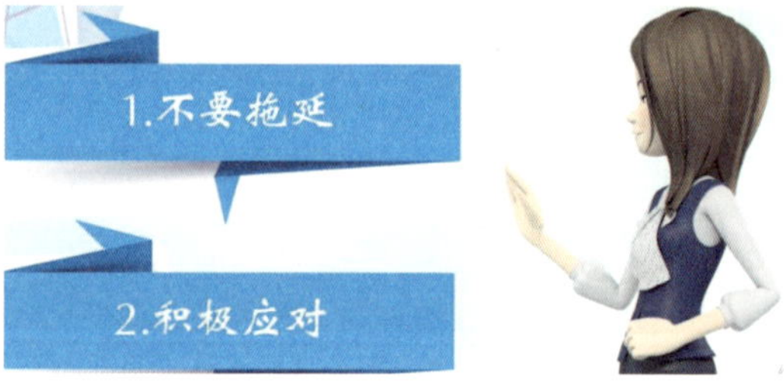

在对外贸易中，双方就订单、合同中的各个条款达成一致意见后，卖方就开始按合同着手执行。但是，买方的市场情况在订单及合同签订后会发生一些变化。为了以后更多的合作，我们选择在可以配合的情况下，尽量配合客人对订单的修订和改变要求。Stella毕业以来一直在金华礼品类出口企业工作，她经手的订单合同大多频率高、数量不大、出货速度较快。这票法国客人的陀螺订单要求在短短的20天内完成出口装运，但客人却两次提出了变更合同的要求。她是如何应对的呢？希望这则小案例能带给大家一些启发和思考。

> 根据上述的介绍，请你完成如下的学习任务：

❶ 归纳客户追加订单时的注意点：

❷ 分析装船前检验发现的问题及起因：

❸ 总结Stella需要承担的责任及处理办法：

❹ 谈谈拓展案例给你的启发：

任务10.4 模拟签订合同的沟通任务

10.4.1 模拟介绍订单信息的任务

出口合同是出口商和进口商后续履约的依据。在这次任务中，我们就订单的前期沟通情况同客户确认合同的主要信息进行汇报。

首先，请简要介绍出口商的背景信息，包括公司或工厂的名称、所属国家等。

其次，汇报双方达成一致意见的主要条款，例如单价、数量、包装、运输方式、装运日期及港口、保险、支付方式等。特别要提醒客户确认和核实双方修改和调整过的有争议的条款。最后，请告知客人订单邮件已发送并请对方及时查收并回复。

【参考例文】

Confirming the Contract

Good morning, this is Cathy Chow from New-star Housewares Import & Export Co., Ltd in China. According to our negotiations, the basic information about Beer Mug with Contract No.BD-239-3-201 comes as follows:

☆ Unit price：1.2 USD/PC CIF Santos

☆ Quantity：16,000 PCS

☆ Packing：one dozen to an egg crated gift box，4 dozens to an export carton，6 cartons to a wooden pallet.

☆ Time of shipment：by Sept. 20th，2018.

☆ Port of departure：Shanghai & Port of destination：Santos

☆ Insurance：to be covered by the seller for 110% of invoice value covering W.P.A.，Risk of Clash & Breakage，and Strike Risk with PICC.

☆ Payment：by D/P at sight.

Please check the terms of packing and port of destination again carefully once more，as we have exchanged different ideas about them for several times. If you have any questions，please contact me as soon as possible. And I have sent you the email at the same time. That's all.

Thank you! Any questions?

› 根据上述的介绍，请你完成如下的学习任务：

记录同学有关合同的汇报要点：

Reporter:	Name of product:
Detailed information	1. 2. 3.
I suggest	
I ask	
I learn	

备注：欢迎大家登录课程的在线平台，点击观看往届学生的任务展示及教师点评。

10.4.2 模拟同客户签约的沟通任务

在这个学习任务中，每个分配到任务的学习小组将根据课程的学习，模拟同客户在签约前进行沟通交流。要求具体如下：

①设计、布置合同签约的沟通表演场景。大家可以考虑如何利用学校及周边的场地进行设置。

②准备相关资料，比如样品、目录册、合同初稿等相关文件资料以及茶水。

③在沟通中：首先，双方审核合同的细节。然后，买家提出存在争议的条款，双方进行协商和沟通。最后，双方修订合同条款并签约。

④请正装出镜。

⑤请在任务中脱稿表演。

> 根据上述的介绍，请你完成如下的学习任务：

记录有关小组签订合同任务的要点：

The team:	Name of product:
Detailed information	1. 2. 3.
I suggest	
I think	
I learn	

备注：欢迎大家登录课程的在线平台，点击观看往届学生的任务展示及教师点评。

10.4.3 模拟沟通签约的即兴任务

在这个任务中，模拟你方与客户就支付展开进一步磋商的工作任务。任务的要点是：首先，买卖双方要把与支付相关的部分信息进行确认。其次，要根据订单的情况对支付方式进行调整。此外，对于支付方式的调整要基于双方的协调和沟通。在本即兴表演中，随机搭配的小组分别扮演客户和卖家，扮演客户的A组要根据自身的利益提出优惠的支付方式并和对方进行协商；扮演卖家的B组要根据订单等实际情况就客人的要求和对方进行协商、合理调整。

> 根据上述的介绍，请你完成如下的学习任务：

❶ 团队根据分配到的任务编号学习相关合同的信息单。

❷ 团队分配任务，根据相关的产品合同信息搜集相关的文字和图片资料并完成准备工作。

❸ 在即兴任务进行时，请在同伴小组的任务单下记录相关的信息并做必要的评价。

即兴任务附件

No.1

Team A (the buyer)

Contract for Porcelain Coffee Set	
Contract No.	YKY5195
Price	US$ 32/set CIF New York
Quantity	6, 000 sets
Packing	1 set/gift box, 12 sets/carton
Insurance	All Risks + Strikes
Payment	60% by T/T, 40% by L/C
Date of shipping	Before Apr. 30
New adjustments	

Team B (the seller)

Contract for Porcelain Coffee Set	
Contract No.	YKY519S
Price	US$ 32/set CIF New York
Quantity	6, 000 sets
Packing	1 set/gift box, 10 sets/carton
Insurance	All Risks + Strikes
Payment	60% by T/T, 40% by L/C
Date of shipping	Before Apr. 30
New adjustments	

No.2

Team A (the buyer)

Contract for Printed Hoodies Sweatshirt	
Contract No.	BVD2167
Price	$7 FOB Ningbo
Quantity	50, 000 PCS
Packing	1 PC/polybag, 60 PCS/carton
Payment	70% by T/T, 30% by L/C
Date of shipping	At the end of May
New adjustments	

Team B (the seller)

Contract for Printed Hoodies Sweatshirt	
Contract No.	BVD2176
Price	$7 FOB Ningbo
Quantity	50, 000 PCS
Packing	1 PC/polybag, 60 PCS/carton
Payment	70% by T/T in advance, 30% by L/C
Date of shipping	At the end of May
New adjustments	

No.3

Team A (the buyer)

Contract for Camp Tent	
Contract No.	CNS6475
Price	USD24 CIF Melbourne
Quantity	1, 500 PCS
Packing	1 piece/fabric bag, 6 PCS in a carton
Insurance	All Risks
Payment	70% by T/T, 30% by L/C
Date of shipping	After Jun. 30
New adjustments	

Team B (the seller)

Contract for Camp Tent	
Contract No.	CNS6475
Price	USD24 CIF Melbourne
Quantity	1, 500 PCS
Packing	1 piece/fabric bag, 6 PCS in a carton
Insurance	All Risks
Payment	30% by T/T, 70% by L/C
Date of shipping	After Jul. 30
New adjustments	

No.4

Team A (the buyer)

Contract for Coffee Maker	
Contract No.	ANH4325
Price	$30 CIF London
Quantity	50, 000 PCS
Packing	1 PC/polybag, 1 DOZ/CTN
Insurance	W.P.A.
Payment	65% by T/T or Western Union, 35% by L/C
Date of shipping	During first half of Dec.
New adjustments	

Team B (the seller)

Contract for Coffee Maker	
Contract No.	ANH4325
Price	$30 CIF London
Quantity	55, 000PCS
Packing	1 PC/polybag, 10 PCS/CTN
Insurance	W.P.A.
Payment	65% by T/T or Western Union, 35% by L/C
Date of shipping	During first half of Dec.
New adjustments	

No.5

Team A (the buyer)

Contract for Spiral Hardcover Notebook	
Contract No.	MKL6584
Price	USD0.5 FOB Shanghai
Quantity	100, 000 PCS
Packing	1 PC into an OPP bag, 60 PCS into double corrugated carton
Payment	60% by T/T, 40% by L/C
Date of shipping	Within 2 weeks
New adjustments	

Team B (the seller)

Contract for Spiral Hardcover Notebook	
Contract No.	KML6548
Price	USD0.5 FOB Shanghai
Quantity	100, 000 PCS
Packing	1 PC into an OPP bag, 50 PCS into double corrugated carton
Payment	70% by T/T, 30% by L/C
Date of shipping	Within 2 weeks
New adjustments	

No.6

Team A (the buyer)

Contract for Plush Lying Dinosaur	
Contract No.	JHF3981
Price	$3 CIF Los Angeles
Quantity	10, 000 PCS
Packing	1 PC/polybag, 4 DOZ/carton
Insurance	W.P.A.
Payment	70% by T/T, 30% by L/C
Date of shipping	On or before Nov. 20
New adjustments	

Team B (the seller)

Contract for Plush Lying Dinosaur	
Contract No.	JHF3981
Price	$3 CIF Los Angeles
Quantity	10, 000 PCS
Packing	1 PC/polybag, 58 PCS/carton
Insurance	W.P.A.
Payment	70% by T/T, 30% by L/C
Date of shipping	On or before Nov. 20
New adjustments	

项目11 沟通海外代理

学习目标

知识目标

1. 了解海外代理分类、优势及注意点；
2. 理解海外代理条件沟通的要点和难点；
3. 掌握海外代理条件的英语表述和沟通策略。

能力目标

1. 能够根据海外代理的主题搜集相关的资料；
2. 掌握如何同目标国客户就海外代理条件进行有效沟通；
3. 明确模拟海外代理条件要点并能够完成情景沟通任务。

任务11.1 认识海外代理

伴随着中国制造的崛起，越来越多的国外市场认可我们的产品，而海外代理也成为一种重要的贸易合作方式。海外代理是由国内的企业（即委托人）与海外代理人签订代理协议，授权海外代理人在一定范围内代表他向第三者进行商品买卖或处理有关事务，海外代理商从中赚取佣金。在海外代理授权时，我们要充分重视代理商的考察、代理类型的选择和代理条件的沟通。

> 根据上述的介绍，请你完成如下的学习任务：

❶ 分析海外代理的优势：

❷ 归纳给予海外代理商的优惠条件：

❸ 列举签订海外代理协议的注意点：

❹ 比较代理的类型：

类型	特点

任务11.2 分析海外代理沟通案例

扫一扫

11.2.1 介绍案例产品：出口晴雨伞

伞是一种遮阳、避雨雪的工具，伞具已由过去功能单一的生活用具发展为花色多样，功能各异，兼有实用性、装饰性的生活必需品。晴雨伞兼具防风防雨、防晒功能，但遮阳、防晒效果相对弱一点。出口企业往往根据目标国消费群体的需求采用不同的伞面、伞骨、设计及测试要求等。目前，晴雨伞的生产基地主要集中在福建晋江、浙江上虞、广东深圳龙岗等地。

> 根据上述的介绍，请你完成如下的学习任务：

❶ 分析伞面的材质：

1.	
2.	
3.	

❷ 比较目标市场的产品偏好：

1.	
2.	
3.	

❸ 列举产品的性能试验：

❹ 总结订单开发和生产的注意点：

扫一扫

11.2.2 海外代理沟通案例

【案例背景介绍】

来自意大利的Angela和Aloha公司一直有贸易往来。今年，Aloha公司研发并推出了一款新材料雨伞，Angela在获取了产品信息后对市场前景充满信心。她提出要求与Aloha公司展开代理合作，双方就代理的相关条款进行沟通。

Angela: Aloha, I want to be your agent in Italy. Your brand is quite popular with our customers. The waterproof fabric umbrella impresses me deeply this year. So it's the right time for us to give it a try.

Aloha: Yes, of course. So far, we have appointed 3 agents in Germany and South Korea. You are our great business partner in Italy, and we appreciate your efforts in pushing sales of our products. So can I have your detailed idea about this?

Angela: Oh, yes. Now we have 20 distributors covering both North and South of Italy. We plan to take more time advertising your products. Our commission shall be paid every 6 months after your agreement.

Aloha: How much is the commission?

Angela: 5%.

Aloha: Ok, we agree. And what else should we offer?

Angela: I need your after-sales service support, then the regular price list and the free samples. I'm respecting that you are making great efforts to give our goods after-sales service.

Aloha: No problem. We can dedicate one colleague who speaks English to give you after-sale service. And we promise the guarantee period up to 3 years. And any question and feedback may be directed to her. Besides, samples will be offered 3–5 times per month and we'll pay for the cost of courier.

Angela: Thanks. I think 2–3 batches of samples per month are more than sufficient.

Aloha: Well. It's great. MOQ (minimum order quantity) should be 2,000 PCS. Can you make it?

Angela: I believe that we can do it for the first year and the quantity will increase for the next year.

Aloha: Great!

Angela: OK, may I know about your collection policy for the goods?

Aloha: How about 100% T/T in advance? I think it will be convenient for both of us.

Angela: We have a long-time cooperation, so can you accept 50%T/T in advance as deposit, and the balance after shipment?

Aloha: 100% T/T in advance is our usual practice. So, I will report to my boss and see if he can handle it as an exception.

Angela: Thank you very much for your help.

Aloha: By the way, how shall we pay you the commission?

Angela: How about PayPal?

Aloha: Yes, we can pay you by PayPal. Now I will prepare the draft of the agency agreement according to our discussion and confirm the payment condition for you meanwhile. So have a short break and take some fruits. Helen!

Helen: Yes.

Aloha: More water for Angela please.

Helen: OK. Please.

Angela: Thank you very much.

Helen: You are welcome.

Aloha: This is the draft of our agency agreement. Please check it and let me know if anything need be revised. As for the payment of goods, I'm afraid I cannot help you.

Angela: If so, then let's keep it as usual this time.

Aloha: Thank you very much for your understanding.

> 根据上述的案例，请你完成如下的学习任务：

❶ 请把加框的单词填入表格并注上中文，并把画线的句子翻译在原文处。

1.	2.	3.	4.
5.	6.	7.	8.

❷ 重点跟读加框的单词、画线的句子并能准确、流利地读出来、说出来。

扫一扫

11.2.3 理解海外代理沟通案例

近年来，中小企业面对国内外严峻的生存环境纷纷转型升级、寻求企业的新竞争力，它们在产品的自主研发、自主设计上获得了国际买家的认可。中小企业的创新力和制造力使得更多的外国客户愿意选择代理方式进行合作。代理的具体条款会涉及哪些？如何磋商？我们在沟通和交流中要注意什么？请大家跟随我们的课程一起进入今天的学习内容。

> 根据上述的介绍，请你完成如下的学习任务：

❶ 分析意大利客户申请代理的原因：

❸ 分析本代理案例的支付方式及其原因：

❹ 谈谈本案例给你的启发：

扫一扫

11.2.4 分析意大利市场及客户

意大利位于欧洲南部，意大利以古老、悠久的文明与艺术闻名于世，是全球拥有世界遗产最多的国家。意大利人总体性格都比较开朗、热情好客。“二战”后意大利积极重建和恢复经济，重新成为发达国家。意大利是中国在欧洲重要的贸易伙伴，越来越多的意大利公司积极开拓中国的巨大市场。中意两国的贸易互补性大于竞争性，在“一带一路”倡议的推动下，两国贸易迎来发展的新机遇。

> 根据上述的介绍，请你完成如下的学习任务：

❶ 列举意大利的概况：

❷ 分析意大利市场特点：

❸ 分析意大利客户特点：

❹ 谈谈本视频给你的启发：

❺ 补充意大利市场及客户分析：

任务11.3 分析海外代理沟通拓展案例

扫一扫

伴随中国制造的崛起，海外的客户越来越认可我们出口的产品。部分海外买家看好产品的市场潜力，愿意通过代理的方式进行合作。在这种出口方式下，代理商可以发挥自身在市场信息和销售渠道方面的优势，出口商也可以通过代理商开拓市场份额，从而实现双赢。Emma在一家中小机电出口公司工作，负责公司在欧美的业务。近年来，欧洲国家的网络设施正在更新换代。在意大利的无线宽带业务发展很快，申请3G/4G的用户不断增加。她的意大利新客人发来邮件，希望成为她公司在意大利的代理。她的公司是如何跟进和应对的呢？希望这则小案例能带给大家一些启发和思考。

> 根据上述的介绍，请你完成如下的学习任务：

❶ 归纳Emma公司应对客户海外代理申请的步骤：

❷ 总结Steven了解客户资质的方法：

❸ 分析双方主要的海外代理条件：

❹ 谈谈拓展案例给你的启发：

任务11.4 模拟海外代理沟通任务

扫一扫

11.4.1 模拟回复老客户代理申请的任务

国外买家对于竞争力强的产品更愿意尝试代理的模式。在任务中，相关同学就老客户的代理申请做出回复。

首先，请简要回顾双方合作的情况，明确可以授予老客户的代理类型。其次，就代理的主要条款，包括产品、区域、期限、支付方式、佣金、销量等给出具体要求。最后，请告知客人代理合同的初稿邮件已发送并请他/她及时查收和回复。

【参考例文】

A Reply to Application of the Exclusive Agency

Hello, Peter. This is Cathy speaking. I leave you a call message according to your application for our sole agency.

We have the three-year cooperation and your orders grow steadily. We have decided to entrust you with the sole agency for the table-cloth in Australia.

The agency agreement will be valid for 2 years. And Minimum Order Quantity is 600,000 PCS each year during the effective period.

The price for each individual transaction shall be fixed through negotiations. We will give you 5% commission of the invoice value. You are supposed to forward market reports every three months.

If you have any questions or new requests, please call me. I have sent you the draft of exclusive agency agreement by email and please check and reply to me soon. That's all.

Thank you! Any questions?

> **根据上述的介绍，请你完成如下的学习任务：**

记录同学有关海外代理汇报要点：

Reporter:	Name of product:
Detailed information	1. 2. 3.
I suggest	
I ask	
I learn	

备注：欢迎大家登录课程的在线平台，点击观看往届学生的任务展示及教师点评。

11.4.2 模拟就新客户代理申请沟通的任务

在这个学习任务中，每个分配到任务的学习小组将根据课程的学习，模拟商讨代理协议的任务。要求具体如下：

①设计、布置面对面、电话或者视频的沟通表演场景。大家可以考虑如何利用学校及周边的场地进行设置。

②准备相关资料，比如代理协议、新客户的背景信息等。

③在沟通中：首先，客户方面就代理协议提出具体要求，包括佣金、支付方式、区域以及相关支持；出口商则要结合客户的背景信息、市场前景以及货物价值等，就销售额、期限、市场报告等条款和客户进行商议。最后，双方就双方关心的上述条款通过沟通最后达成意向。

④请正装出镜；请在任务中脱稿表演。

> 根据上述的介绍，请你完成如下的学习任务：

记录有关小组沟通代理任务的要点：

The team:	Name of product:
Detailed information	1. 2. 3.
I suggest	
I ask	
I learn	

备注：欢迎大家登录课程的在线平台，点击观看往届学生的任务展示及教师点评。

扫一扫

11.4.3 模拟沟通海外代理的即兴任务

在这个任务中，模拟你方与客户就代理合同展开进一步磋商的工作任务。任务的要点是：首先，要把代理合同中的部分条款通过进一步协商加以确认；其次，要根据各自的实际情况对合同条款进行协商。在本即兴表演中，随机搭配的小组分别扮演代理商和委托企业的经理，扮演国外代理商的A组可能要根据自身的资质对代理的条款提出协商和调整的要求；扮演委托企业的经理B组可能根据企业的经验和销售目标同代理商就部分条款进行协商和合理调整。

> **根据上述的介绍，请你完成如下的学习任务：**

❶ 团队根据分配到的任务编号学习相关的海外代理的信息单。

❷ 团队分配任务，根据相关的海外代理信息搜集相关的文字和图片资料并完成准备工作。

❸ 在即兴任务进行时，请在同伴小组的任务单下记录相关的信息并做必要的评价。

即兴任务附件

No.1

Team A (the agent)

Exclusive Agency for Solar Water Heater	
Article No.	SS2018-31
Price	each transaction shall be fixed by negotiations
Payment	confirmed, irrevocable L/C
Minimum order quantity	( ) containers each year (40 HQ)
Period	year(s)
Territory	North Europe
Market reports	Every __4__ months
New adjustments	

Team B (the principal)

Exclusive Agency for Solar Water Heater	
Article No.	SS2018-31
Price	each transaction shall be fixed by negotiations
Payment	confirmed, irrevocable L/C
Minimum order quantity	(12) containers each year (40 HQ)
Period	1 year
Area	Denmark
Market reports	Every __ months
New adjustments	

No.2

Team A (the agent)

Sole Agency for Pure Silk Quilt	
Article No.	CC2016–21
Price	each transaction shall be fixed by negotiations
Payment	By 100% T/T
Minimum order quantity	( ) containers each year (20 GP)
Period	____ year(s)
Territory	America
Market reports	Every ___ months
New adjustments	

Team B (the principal)

Sole Agency for Pure Silk Quilt	
Article No.	CC2016–21
Price	each transaction shall be fixed by negotiations
Payment	
Minimum order quantity	24 containers each year (20 GP)
Period	__2__ years
Territory	America
Market reports	Every ___ months
New adjustments	

No.3

Team A (the agent)

Sole Agency for Wireless Alarm System	
Article No.	AF2005-15
Payment	By confirmed, irrevocable L/C
Minimum order quantity	
Duration	___ year(s)
Territory	India
Commission	___% of the net invoiced selling price of products
Market reports	Every ___ months
New adjustments	

Team B (the principal)

Sole Agency for Wireless Alarm System	
Article No.	AF2005-15
Payment	By confirmed, irrevocable L/C
Minimum order quantity	500, 000 sets each year
Duration	__2__ years
Territory	India
Commission	3.5% of the net invoiced selling price of products
Market reports	Every __3__ months
New adjustments	

No.4

Team A (the agent)

Sole Agency for Under-counter Dishwasher	
Article No.	DV2011-16
Payment	By T/T
Minimum order quantity	( ) containers each year
Duration	___ year(s)
Territory	Britain
Commission	__% of the net invoiced selling price of products
Place of arbitration	Hong Kong
New adjustments	

Team B (the principal)

Sole Agency for Under-counter Dishwasher	
Article No.	DV2011-16
Payment	By T/T
Minimum order quantity	( ) containers each year
Duration	__2__ years
Territory	Britain
Commission	5.5% of the net invoiced selling price of products
Place of arbitration	Hong Kong
New adjustments	

No.5

Team A (the agent)

Non-exclusive Agency for Mini Car Fridge	
Article No.	KL2011-36
Payment	By T/T
Minimum order quantity	3, 000 PCS each year
Duration	___ year(s)
Territory	Australia
Commission	6% of the net invoiced selling price of products
Market reports	Every __3__ months
New adjustments	

Team B (the principal)

Non-exclusive Agency for Mini Car Fridge	
Article No.	KL2011-36
Payment	By L/C
Minimum order quantity	5, 000 PCS each year
Duration	___ year(s)
Territory	Australia
Commission	5% of the net invoiced selling price of products
Market reports	Every __4__ months
New adjustments	

No.6

Team A (the agent)

General Agency for Lady City Bike	
Article No.	BB2015-41
Price	each transaction shall be fixed by negotiations
Payment	By T/T in advance
Minimum order quantity	10, 000 PCS each year
Period	3 years
Territory	France
Commission	__% of the net invoiced selling price of products
New adjustments	

Team B (the principal)

General Agency for Lady City Bike	
Article No.	BB2015-41
Price	each transaction shall be fixed by negotiations
Payment	Confirmed, irrevocable L/C
Minimum order quantity	15, 000 PCS each year
Period	2 years
Territory	France
Commission	__% of the net invoiced selling price of products
New adjustments	

项目12 沟通客户投诉

学习目标

知识目标

1. 了解客户投诉的原因、处理方法和注意点；
2. 理解处理投诉沟通的要点和难点；
3. 掌握应对客户投诉及索赔的英语表述和沟通策略。

能力目标

1. 能够根据客户投诉的主题搜集相关的资料；
2. 掌握如何同目标国客户就投诉展开有效沟通；
3. 明确模拟处理投诉任务的要点并完成情景模拟任务。

任务12.1 认识客户投诉

扫一扫

一般而言，国外的客户会因实际货物和合同中订立的要求有偏差向出口企业提出投诉。面对客户的投诉，我们要积极应对、主动跟进，客观、敬业、用心地处理客户提出的投诉及要求。同时，我们也要转变心态和观念，正确识别和挖掘客户投诉带给出口企业的价值：比如修正出口产品及服务，提升企业的海外形象，培养国外客户的忠诚度，挖掘国外市场潜在的商机。

> 根据上述的介绍，请你完成如下的学习任务：

❶ 总结客户投诉的原因：

1.	
2.	
3.	
4.	

❷ 归纳处理客户投诉的态度：

❸ 分析应对客户投诉的方法：

❹ 列举处理客户投诉的注意点：

任务12.2 分析客户投诉沟通案例

扫一扫

12.2.1 介绍案例产品：出口毛绒玩具

毛绒玩具（plush toy），也可以称为软性玩具（soft toy）、填充玩具（stuffed toy），以毛绒面料与PP棉及其他纺织材料为主要面料，内部填塞各种填充物而制成的玩具。毛绒玩具属于非生活必需品，其出口市场和出口量取决于目标国或地区的经济水平以及家庭的消费能力。同时，面对目标市场不断完善的安全法规、法令，毛绒玩具在出口中应特别注意产品的安全性。

> 根据上述的介绍，请你完成如下的学习任务：

❶ 分析毛绒玩具的面料：

❷ 列举毛绒玩具的填充物：

❸ 分析出口的安全要求：

1.	
2.	
3.	

❹ 总结企业提升出口竞争力的路径：

12.2.2 客户投诉沟通案例

【案例背景介绍】

澳大利亚的客户Robyn和Jonas的公司一直有贸易往来。最近，Robyn从Jonas公司采购的玩具在市场销售中因品质问题遭到了消费者投诉及退货。Robyn第一时间联系了Jonas，Jonas根据她的反馈提出了相应的补偿方案，最后双方达成了和解。

Robyn: Good morning. This is Robyn speaking.

Jonas: Good morning, it's very nice to talk with you. How can I help you?

Robyn: I am calling to inform you that the plush toys you sent last month are available for sale now, but several customers have returned the goods.

Jonas: What's wrong? Please tell me in details.

Robyn: I have contacted with the retailers and their feedback shows that this batch of goods is surprisingly inferior in quality.

Jonas: Oh, I'm so sorry to hear that. This is the first time that our goods have been returned in the foreign markets. We will pay full attention to this batch of goods.

Robyn: Yeah, Jonas. We have cooperated together for 3 years. I cannot believe this at first.

Jonas: I'm sorry for the trouble. Can you show me some of the goods returned by your customers?

Robyn: Yes, wait for a moment. I have the pictures and I will send you now.

Jonas: Thanks. Ok, I have downloaded them.

Robyn: In the first picture, you can see a hole. And in the second picture, the seam is open. In the third picture, this toy is poorly trimmed. And in the last one, the toy is deformed.

Jonas: Yes, I admit that the quality is not up to our standard. We're sorry to bring you so much inconvenience.

Robyn: Yes, I have to say we are now in a terrible situation.

Jonas: Robyn, we are old friends. I have to say this event is terrible but please trust us. We will give you some discount according to the defectives.

Robyn: Discount?

Jonas: As for the major defectives like broken holes, open seams and so on, we will offer you a 20% discount; as for the minor defectives, like untrimmed thread ends we will offer a 5% discount. Please tell us the quantity of defective goods and we'll pay you the compensation.

Robyn: Well, I think your suggestions are quite reasonable.

Jonas: We can deduct the amount from your next batch of goods if it's acceptable to you.

Robyn: Fine. I agree with you.

Jonas: I will look into the order and send you the findings.

Robyn: Great, Jonas. In this way, we can avoid such returns in the future.

Jonas: I sincerely apologize for the quality issue again and thank you very much for trusting us, and accepting our solutions.

Robyn: Anyway, we have cooperated with each other for a long time.

Jonas: If there is anything you need, please let me know, Robyn.

Robyn: Well, I will. Have a great day! Bye!

Jonas: Thanks for calling and bye.

> 根据上述的案例，请你完成如下的学习任务：

❶ 请把加框的单词填入表格并注上中文，并把画线的句子翻译在原文处。

1.	2.	3.	4.
5.	6.	7.	8.

❷ 重点跟读加框的单词、画线的句子并能准确、流利地读出来、说出来。

扫一扫

12.2.3 理解客户投诉沟通案例

我们出口到国外市场的订单多了之后，不可避免会出现一些问题。我们的货物如果确实存在客户投诉的相关问题，主动担当是我们应该采取的态度，一个有求无应的供应商迟早会为客户所抛弃。面对客户的投诉如何积极应对？如何把客户投诉转变成企业品质和管理的提升呢？如何在处理投诉过程中展现优质的售后服务？我们在沟通和交流中要注意什么？请大家跟随我们的课程一起进入今天的学习内容。

> 根据上述的介绍，请你完成如下的学习任务：

❶ 列举 Robyn 投诉的产品问题（英文即可）：

1.	
2.	
3.	
4.	

❷ 归纳Jonas给出的赔偿方案：

❸ 分析Jonas在应对投诉时的方法：

❹ 谈谈本案例给予你的启发：

扫一扫

12.2.4 分析澳大利亚市场及客户

澳大利亚资源丰富，是南半球经济最发达的国家，被誉为“The lucky country”。农牧业、采矿业是澳大利亚的传统产业，近年来澳大利亚的高科技产业发展较快。澳大利亚是典型的移民国家，澳大利亚人办事认真、爽快，待人诚恳、开朗、热情，而且特别喜爱体育运动。澳大利亚外贸依存度大，中国是澳大利亚主要贸易伙伴之一。中澳两国贸易互补性很强，双方的经贸合作具有广阔的发展空间。

> 根据上述的介绍，请你完成如下的学习任务：

❶ 列举澳大利亚的概况：

❷ 分析澳大利亚市场特点：

❸ 分析澳大利亚客户特点：

❹ 谈谈本视频给你的启发：

❺ 补充澳大利亚市场及客户分析：

任务12.3 分析客户投诉沟通拓展案例

扫一扫

在订单的执行过程中，我们可能会因为工期、品质、包装等不符合要求而遭遇投诉。面对客户的投诉，我们要以敬业的精神分析问题，提出可行的解决方案，而不是推脱和逃避。积极应对投诉并提出合理的解决方案，体现了外贸人的职业素养、经验和价值。Cathy就职于一家中小型服装出口公司，她经手的这票3000 PCS女式连衣裙被安排在2017年5月10日装船出口到俄罗斯，客人5月5日到工厂实施检验后发现拉链处的蕾丝不符合要求，要求进行整改并要求货物打8.5折。她是如何处理客户投诉的呢？希望这则案例能带给大家一些思考和启发。

› 根据上述的介绍，请你完成如下的学习任务：

❶ 归纳俄罗斯客户投诉的问题：

❷ 分析工厂对俄罗斯客户索赔的态度：

❸ 总结Cathy的整改方案：

❹ 谈谈拓展案例给予你的启发：

任务12.4 模拟客户投诉沟通任务

12.4.1 模拟应对装运前遭投诉的沟通任务

产品在出口过程中可能会遭遇各种投诉，其中在客人对装运前的货物实施检验的过程中就会发现各种问题并要求卖家解决，比如包装不当、品质有问题等等。在任务中，相关同学就客检后客人的投诉做出回复。

首先，请简要回顾买家投诉的问题以及调查结果。其次，根据客户反映的问题以及要求，给出解决方案。最后，再次表达歉意并表明下不为例，期待客人的回复。

【参考例文】

A Reply to My Client's Claims

Dear Lydia, this is Jack speaking.

I got your message about your claims on Order No.455 against us. You told us that the color fastness of T-shirts is not up to the level. I have contacted our factory and informed it of your dissatisfaction. They felt very sorry for this and explained that they couldn't control the color fastness.

We apologize for any inconvenience caused. Maybe we can change the washing instructions from "Water" to "Dry Clean". And we will pay for the cost. Besides, we will give you 2% discount. We will take all possible steps to avoid any recurrence in our dealings with you.

Dear Lydia, if there is anything I can do for you, please let me know. If you have any questions or new requests, please call me. That's all.

Thank you! Any questions?

> **根据上述的介绍，请你完成如下的学习任务：**

记录同学有关海外代理的汇报要点：

Reporter:	Name of product:
Detailed information	1. 2. 3.
I suggest	
I ask	
I learn	

备注：欢迎大家登录课程的在线平台，点击观看往届学生的任务展示及教师点评。

12.4.2 模拟应对客户售后投诉的沟通任务

在这个学习任务中，每个分配到任务的学习小组将根据课程的学习，模拟处理客户售后投诉的任务。要求具体如下：

①设计、布置面对面、电话或者视频的沟通表演场景。大家可以考虑如何利用学校及周边的场地进行设置。

②准备相关资料，比如：客户提供的资料、样品、合同等。

③在沟通中：首先，双方核实客户投诉的问题及细节。然后，找出原因和相关的责任方。最后，卖家和客户协商并给出合理的解决方案。

④请正装出镜；请在任务中脱稿表演。

> 根据上述的介绍，请你完成如下的学习任务：

记录有关小组应对投诉任务的要点：

The team:	Name of product:
Detailed information	1. 2. 3.
I suggest	
I think	
I learn	

备注：欢迎大家登录课程的在线平台，点击观看往届学生的任务展示及教师点评。

扫一扫

12.4.3 模拟应对投诉的即兴任务

在这个任务中，模拟如何解决客户提出的投诉问题。任务的要点是：首先，我们要了解客人会因为订单执行不力而可能提出的各种投诉；其次，买家重在把投诉情况说清楚，卖家要根据买家提供的信息进行核实并提出合理的解决和赔偿方案。在本即兴表演中，随机搭配的小组分别扮演客户和卖家，扮演客户的A组要把投诉的情况说清楚，提出自己的要求；扮演卖家的B组要根据实际情况提出可行的方案并和客户进行协商。

> 根据上述的介绍，请你完成如下的学习任务：

❶ 团队根据分配到的任务编号学习相关的客户投诉信息单。

❷ 团队分配任务，根据相关的客户投诉信息搜集相关的文字和图片资料并完成准备工作。

❸ 在即兴任务进行时，请在同伴小组的任务单下记录相关的信息并做必要的评价。

即兴任务附件

No.1

Team A (the buyer)

The Case of Men Leather Sports Gloves	
Contract No.	YKY5195A
Quantity	15, 000 pairs
Expected color	black
Color delivered	brown
Compensation	
Reasons	
Final solution	

Team B (the seller)

The Case of Men Leather Sports Gloves	
Contract No.	YKY5195A
Quantity	15, 000 pairs
Expected color	black
Color delivered	brown
Solutions	
Final solution	

No.2

Team A (the buyer)

The Case of Cotton Baby Cloak	
Contract No.	KS29053
Unit price	USD4.2/PC CIF Hamburg
Expected Qty.	5, 868 PCS
Qty. delivered	5, 865 PCS
Compensation	
Reasons	
Final solution	

Team B (the seller)

The Case of Cotton Baby Cloak	
Contract No.	KS29053
Unit price	USD4.2/PC CIF Hamburg
Expected Qty.	5, 868 PCS
Qty. delivered	5, 865 PCS
Solutions	
Final solution	

No.3

Team A (the buyer)

The Case of Women Fashion Slippers	
Contract No.	KSPP-8007
Unit price	USD2.5/pair CIF Seattle, 50, 000 pairs
Time of case	3 days before shipping
Expected packing	One pair with an OPP bag, 20 pairs in a big OPP bag, 80 pairs in a carton
Actual packing	20 pairs in a big OPP bag, 80 pairs in a carton
Compensation	
Reasons	
Final solution	

Team B (the seller)

The Case of Women Fashion Slippers	
Contract No.	KSPP-8007
Unit price	USD2.5/pair CIF Seattle, 50, 000 pairs
Time of case	3 days before shipping
Expected Packing	One pair with an OPP bag, 20 pairs in a big OPP bag, 80 pairs in a carton
Actual packing	20 pairs in a big OPP bag, 80 pairs in a carton
Solutions	
Final solution	

No.4

Team A (the buyer)

The Case of Promotional Sports Sweatband	
Contract No.	NK2011–23
Unit price	USD1.5/PC CIF Singapore
Total amount	USD8, 000
Expected delivery	Before May 10 by sea
Would-be delivery	Before Jun. 1st
Compensation	
Reasons	
Final solution	

Team B (the seller)

The Case of Promotional Sports Sweatband	
Contract No.	NK2011–23
Unit price	USD1.5/PC CIF Singapore
Total amount	USD8, 000
Expected delivery	Before May 10 by sea
Would-be delivery	Before Jun. 1st
Solutions	
Final solution	

No.5

Team A (the buyer)

The Case of Crystal Glass Trophy	
Contract No.	GW–KSD01W
Expected transport	LCL is not allowed
Actual transport	LCL
Results	30% of goods are broken
Compensation	
Reasons	
Final solution	

Team B (the seller)

The Case of Crystal Glass Trophy	
Contract No.	GW–KSD01W
Expected transport	LCL is not allowed
Actual transport	LCL
Results	30% of goods are broken
Solutions	
Final solution	

No.6

Team A (the buyer)

The Case of Summer Women Dress	
Contract No.	LKM40201
Material	100% Cotton
Expected dimensional stability	Within 5%
Actual dimensional stability	More than 7%
Compensation	
Reasons	
Final solution	

Team B (the seller)

The Case of Summer Women Dress	
Contract No.	LKM40201
Material	100% Cotton
Expected dimensional stability	Within 5%
Actual dimensional stability	More than 7%
Solutions	
Final solution	